ENDORSEMENTS

Leaving Ordinary is a study well-suited for the disciple who is yearning for more than just the ordinary in prayer time. Drawing from the lessons of Donna Gaines' own life journey, and using the tabernacle along with its articles, the reader will gain insight and knowledge of the intimate pursuit that our God has had for each of us since the beginning of time. Every disciple serious about an intimate relationship with our God needs to complete this study.

> **—Diane Nix**
> Pastor's Wife, Mom, Founder of ContagiousJoy4him.com,
> Author, Speaker/Teacher

Donna Gaines unveils the mysteries of the tabernacle to reveal the intimacy available to anyone who dares to approach the Holy of Holies. Through personal stories and detailed insights, what was once complex suddenly becomes a familiar journey alongside so great a Savior. Page by page, you will find yourself eager to "enter in" to His presence.

> **—Diane Strack**
> Author, *The Journals of Mary* and *Fresh Start for Single Moms*

As you read this book on the tabernacle, God will use the principles and pictures to once again fan the flames of the Spirit's fire that resides within you.

> **—Johnny Hunt**
> Former President, Southern Baptist Convention
> Pastor, First Baptist Church Woodstock, GA

Every believer knows the importance of prayer, however every believer has not experienced how prayer can transform a believer's life. Donna Gaines is not content with going through the motions when it comes to prayer. In *Leaving Ordinary*, Donna uses the tabernacle and its articles as a guide to show believers how to experience true intimacy with

God through prayer. I assure you that your prayer life will be transformed as you leave the ordinary!"

—**Fred Luter Jr.**
Pastor, Franklin Avenue Baptist Church, New Orleans, LA
President, Southern Baptist Convention

If you desire to live a life wholly committed to prayer and worship, you need to read Donna Gaines' newest book that was born out of her personal experience and pursuit of true worship. This book can serve as a template that will guide you to "leave ordinary" and experience the power and presence of God extraordinarily.

—**Jeana Floyd**
Author, *Uninvited Guest* and *10 Things Every Minister's Wife Needs to Know*

With clarity and candor Donna Gaines walks us through the Old Testament tabernacle, the house of God, and a beautiful type of our Lord Jesus Christ in his Person and work. Join her as with personal insights, family illustrations, and genuine inspiration she leads you through the thrilling truths of God's house. Your life will no longer be ordinary but will be transformed into the extraordinary.

—**Heather Olford**
Widow of Dr. Stephen F. Olford and author of *Together with God*

Donna Gaines brings the reader with her as she journeys through the Tabernacle, discovering fresh insights into prayer and one's walk with God. When applied, these truths really do move the believer out of the "ordinary" and into an "extraordinary" prayer life. Your heart will be warmed as your find fresh intimacy with God through the study of the Tabernacle.

—**Susie Hawkins**
Author, *From One Ministry Wife to Another*

LEAVING ORDINARY

ENCOUNTER GOD
through
EXTRAORDINARY PRAYER

DONNA GAINES

THOMAS NELSON
Since 1798

NASHVILLE   DALLAS   MEXICO CITY   RIO DE JANEIRO

Published in Nashville, Tennessee, by Thomas Nelson. Thomas Nelson is a trademark of HarperCollins Christian Publishing, Inc.

Page design and layout: Crosslin Creative

Illustrations by Mark C. Alexander

Thomas Nelson, Inc., titles may be purchased in bulk for educational, business, fund-raising, or sales promotional use. For information, please e-mail SpecialMarkets@ ThomasNelson.com.

Unless otherwise noted, Scripture quotations are taken from The Voice™ translation. © 2012 Ecclesia Bible Society. Used by permission. All rights reserved.˙

Note: Italics in quotations from The Voice are used to "indicate words not directly tied to the dynamic translation of the original language" but that "bring out the nuance of the original, assist in completing ideas, and . . . provide readers with information that would have been obvious to the original audience" (The Voice, preface). Emphasis in quotations from The Voice is indicated with the use of **boldface** type.

Scripture quotations marked ESV are taken from THE ENGLISH STANDARD VERSION. © 2001 by Crossway Bibles, a division of Good News Publishers.

Scripture quotations marked KJV are taken from the Holy Bible, King James Version (public domain).

Scripture quotations marked MSG are taken from *The Message* by Eugene H. Peterson. © 1993, 1994, 1995, 1996, 2000. Used by permission of NavPress Publishing Group. All rights reserved.

Scripture quotations marked NASB are taken from the NEW AMERICAN STANDARD BIBLE®, © The Lockman Foundation 1960, 1962, 1963, 1968, 1971, 1972, 1973, 1975, 1977, 1995. Used by permission.

Scripture quotations marked NIV are taken from the Holy Bible, New International Version®, NIV®. Copyright © 1973, 1978, 1984, 2011 by Biblica, Inc.™ Used by permission of Zondervan. All rights reserved worldwide. www.zondervan.com.

Scripture quotations marked NLT are from the *Holy Bible*, New Living Translation. © 1996, 2004, 2007. Used by permission of Tyndale House Publishers, Inc., Carol Stream, Illinois 60188. All rights reserved.

Scripture quotations marked NKJV are taken from the NEW KING JAMES VERSION. © 1982 by Thomas Nelson. Used by permission. All rights reserved.

Scripture quotations marked TLB are taken from *The Living Bible*. © 1971. Used by permission of Tyndale House Publishers, Inc., Wheaton, Illinois 60189. All rights reserved.

Scripture quotations marked YLT are taken from Young's Literal Translation (public domain).

ISBN: 9781401679699

Printed in the United States of America

14 15 16 17 18 19 RRD 6 5 4 3 2

To

My daughters and daughter-in-law

Lindsey

Allison

Bethany

Melisa

So grateful for your love for Jesus and your faithfulness to "enter in." May you never settle for ordinary when such an extraordinary God indwells you!

ACKNOWLEDGMENTS

To Maleah Bell, thank you for your editorial assistance but most importantly for your friendship. To the great team at Thomas Nelson, thank you for your vision and enthusiasm for InScribed.

A great big thanks goes to the M Club—my sweet friends and prayer warriors. Thank you for Nashville, for the many prayers, e-mails and words of encouragement. Dayna and Joni, thank you for the sacrifice of your time and your help with the manuscript. You all are the best!

To the women of Gardendale FBC (where God first revealed these truths) and Bellevue Baptist Church for the joy of journeying toward home with you! What a delight to experience Him in community with all of you!

To my family—thank you for your prayers and support. And thank you for your understanding and encouragement! I am most blessed!!

To Steve—thank you for allowing me to fulfill the call that God has placed on my life. I am a better woman because of you. Thank you for your faithfulness to God's Word and prayer. You challenge me!

Forgive me for being so ordinary while
claiming to know so extraordinary a God.

—Jim Elliot

CONTENTS

❧ Part Three ❧

PREFACE

In Ecclesiastes 3:11, Solomon wisely stated that God has "set eternity in [our] hearts" (NKJV). This internal awareness and longing to "know" God and to experience Him has caused me to seek Him with increasing fervency as I have grown in my relationship with Him. Over the years, there have been a few times in my seeking that God's manifest presence has seemed almost overwhelmingly tangible.

One of those times was in March 2003, when I was teaching a Bible study on the book of Exodus. Early one Saturday morning, I went to the special place where I meet with the Lord every day. After reading my Bible, I knelt in front of my favorite chair and spread my prayer notebook out on the ottoman. My thoughts kept returning to the tabernacle, the topic I was preparing to teach the next week. My mind was reeling with all that the Lord had been revealing to me. Not only was God going to dwell among His people, but every article of the tabernacle pointed to a heavenly reality and to ultimate fulfillment in Jesus Christ.

I was suddenly enveloped by the Lord's presence, and I began to weep. As I quieted my heart, I sensed the Lord saying to me, *"Walk with Me. Minister to Me in the tabernacle not made with human hands."* God was inviting me to serve Him just as the priests of old had done. With my heart pounding and tears streaming, I went from article to article in the tabernacle as the Lord revealed how its pattern could be a guide to prepare my heart to minister to Him in prayer. There was a progression the priests had to follow before entering the Holy of Holies, and I could follow that same pattern to prepare my heart to pray according to His will. Just like Moses, I could enter into the presence of the Most High.

That morning my *ordinary* daily practice of prayer became an *extraordinary encounter* with the living God. This life-transforming practice remains a vital part of my time with the Lord. In the years that have passed, I have taught the truths the Lord revealed to me that day to small groups, to weekly Bible study groups, and to women at conferences and retreats.

The intimacy I experienced that day is what God desires for each of us. He has made His longing for relationship evident since the beginning of time. He has gone to great lengths to reveal Himself and to allow us to experience Him. Using the tabernacle and its articles as a guide, it is possible to minister to, or serve, God in the secret place of true intimacy that leads to worship. Through prayer we are granted access to the very throne of God (Heb. 4:16). As we spend time in His presence, He will begin to reveal to us truths from His Word and open our heart and eyes to "see" Him as never before.

As finite humans, we desire models to explain the workings of the world around us—the tabernacle is God's concrete representation of the unseen heavenly reality where He dwells (Heb. 8:5; 9:24). We desperately long for models to help us "see" what we are told to believe. But it is in believing when we *can't* see that God grants us spiritual sight and revelation.

God gave the instructions for the tabernacle during the Hebrews' desert wanderings. He granted them the ability to "see" His presence in the wilderness through the pillar of cloud and fire. In a very visible, tangible way, God was saying, *Walk with Me. Leave "ordinary"—what you have always known—and enter into an* extraordinary *relationship with Me. A relationship in which you will be challenged* to *"walk by faith, not by sight"* (2 Cor. 5:7 NASB). God wants that kind of relationship with you too, a relationship that creates a new "normal," not based on your physical senses, but on His Spirit. A relationship steeped in His Word and prayer through which you experience His presence.

This extraordinary relationship leads to a stress-free life. In Philippians 4:6–7, we are commanded to be "anxious for nothing" (NKJV). But how are we to do this? By trusting the One who has called us and is preparing us for heaven. I did not say that you would have a pain-free or trouble-free life. Jesus said just the opposite. He said, "In the world you have tribulation," then added, "but take courage; I have overcome the world" (John 16:33 NASB).

If He has overcome, we can overcome *through* Him! The Spirit of God has the ability to lift you above the circumstances of your life so you begin to see them from an eternal vantage point. That means taking the intrusive thoughts of anxiety and worry that seem to bombard your mind at times and refusing them entrance. Second Corinthians 10:5 tells us to take "every thought captive to the obedience of Christ" (NASB).

Instead of worrying, turn those anxious thoughts into prayer requests. Jesus has told us to "cast all [our] anxiety on him because he cares for [us]" (1 Peter 5:7 NIV). As we do this, we can claim His peace that will build a fortress around our hearts and minds. Then Isaiah 26:3 will become a reality: "You will keep in perfect peace all who trust in you, all whose thoughts are fixed on you!" (NLT).

We are not to live as "mere men" (1 Cor. 3:3 NASB). We leave "ordinary" behind when we meet Christ and begin to live the Spirit life that only He can provide. As we look to Jesus, He says to us what He said to the Israelites in the wilderness:

- *Walk with Me and I will show you the way.*

- *Walk with Me and I will provide for your needs.*

- *Walk with Me and I will give you rest.*

The Old Testament tabernacle is our model for worship. We will discover in this study that Jesus is the New Testament model for living. He was God's "in the flesh" invitation to "walk with Me" and experience this extraordinary relationship with God through Christ. His disciples walked with Him, and as they did, they learned how to live. Like Christ's disciples, we will find that it is only after we have truly worshipped that we are able to really live. One day we will join Jesus, our "high priest [who is . . .] right alongside God, conducting worship in the one true sanctuary built by God" (Heb. 8:2 MSG).

As I wait for that day, my heart is still captured by the truths of the tabernacle, and I pray yours will be too!

Donna Gaines
2014

The Anointed One did not enter into handcrafted sacred spaces—imperfect copies of heavenly originals—but into heaven itself, where He stands in the presence of God on our behalf.

—Hebrews 9:24

PART ONE

THE STORY BEHIND THE TABERNACLE

When we study the Bible in its entirety, we see the big picture. The Bible is God's revelation of His character and His pursuit of humankind in spite of our rebellious nature. As Henri Nouwen so beautifully stated, "The story of Christ is . . . not the 'greatest story ever told', but the only story ever told. It is the story from which all other stories receive their meaning and significance. The story of Christ makes history real."[1] And the story of Christ makes our stories real and significant.

The scarlet thread of redemption can be traced throughout the Bible. Every individual story contained in the Bible is really telling one story—the overarching story of God's pursuit of humankind, which culminated in the sacrifice of His Son. Thus, it is through the Promised One of Genesis 3:15 that we may enter into relationship with God the Father.

There is no real understanding of the gospel apart from this grasp of the Grand Narrative. *The Story* gives meaning to our individual stories. God's desire for relationship with humankind is the truth that permeates God's Story from beginning to end. He is the God who reveals Himself to those who seek Him with their whole hearts (Jer. 29:13).

CHAPTER ONE

GOD'S WORD

All of Scripture is God-breathed; *in its* inspired *voice, we hear* useful teaching, rebuke, correction, *instruction, and* training for a life that is right.

—2 Timothy 3:16

Shortly after our fourth child was born, I was longing for my time with the Lord. After the birth of each of my children, there was a significant adjustment period. My orderly world had been turned upside down. Trying to keep a household going for my pastor husband and four children (ranging from newborn to ten) while sleep deprived proved to be beyond me. I cried out to the Lord as I trudged through my days. I remember walking into my laundry room one day and just turning around and walking back out—too overwhelmed to tackle the mountain that faced me.

A couple of days after the laundry episode, I returned to our Tuesday morning women's Bible study. My newborn was three weeks old. I was lonely and looking forward to adult conversation. But what I was really longing for was a word from the Lord.

Driving back to the house, I felt somewhat uplifted, but still yearning. I stopped routinely at the mailbox as I pulled into our driveway and found a package. Denise George had sent me her recently published book, *A Longing Heart Hears God's Gentle Whisper.* The words jumped out at me as though I had received a postcard from heaven!

About three o'clock the next morning, as I was up nursing my baby, I opened the book. I just "happened" to open to a section where the author was comparing the miracle of prayer to the miracle of a newborn baby. As I looked at the delicate features of our little girl and then back at the book, I read these words:

> Imagine! Through prayer, you and I can call upon the One who fashioned our delicate bodies, who gifted our hearts and minds. The One who created us and gave us breath! The One who listens to us, our prayers of thanks and our prayers of complaints. The One who loves us so deeply that He would rather die than live without us.[1]

At that moment, the presence of The One filled the little nursery where I rocked my baby, and I was overwhelmed by His love. His love! Not reprimand because I hadn't been having my quiet time, but love, pure and unrestrained. My heart began to pound and tears began to flow. He loves me! He heard and He saw me. I thought my heart might burst right open. His goodness had filled that room, and I was at once both comforted and encouraged.

Dear friend (I hope I can call you that since I have prayed for those who would read this book, and I feel that we are friends), this same intimacy and awareness are what God desires for each of His children to experience. Perhaps God may seem distant to you, as He did to me. Or maybe you aren't convinced His promises include you. But I can tell you from personal experience, the only One who can satisfy is seeking you!

The way you get to know Him is through His Word. The Bible is God's autobiography. It is written by God, about God, for us.

This is not just any book. It is God-breathed and living and has the power to breathe new life into your soul. Read through it slowly and intentionally. Expect God to speak to you. When God begins to reveal a specific truth to you, you can't look at the Scriptures without seeing it. When you pick up the Bible, He will reinforce that same truth on page after page.

> The Bible is God's auto-biography. It is written by God, about God, for us.

Do you remember Magic Eye pictures? They were images created by lines of repeated characters. If you looked intently into the center of the picture—you almost had to cross your eyes—suddenly a hidden image would pop out, actually appearing to come to the surface. After that initial realization, every time you looked at the picture, you saw it. You couldn't help but see it. My sister Julie had a Magic Eyes picture that had a dinosaur hidden in it. It seemed to take me forever to be able to see it. I tilted my head, almost crossed my eyes, and looked intently into the center of the picture. Then, suddenly, I saw it! After that, no matter from what angle I came up to the picture, I saw it. Once you have seen it—you can't *not* see it!

As we work through the Scripture chronologically, we will see over and over again the great lengths to which God was willing to go that He might dwell with His people. Because God desired to have an intimate relationship with them, He gave them instructions for the tabernacle. To understand the significance of the tabernacle as our model for worship and relationship, it will help to look at the big picture of God's story. He longs to be with us. His presence was manifest first in the garden, then when He cut covenant with Abraham, then in the tabernacle, and centuries later in the temple. In the New Testament, He became flesh through His Son, who literally "tabernacle[d]" among us (John 1:14 YLT).

After Christ's ascension, God sent His Holy Spirit so that "whoever believes in Him will not face everlasting destruction, but will have everlasting life" (John 3:16). Those who believe are indwelt by His Spirit. It is the same Spirit that indwelled the tabernacle in the wilderness, the temple in Jerusalem, and Christ Himself.

And now, Christ is preparing for the day when nothing will separate us from His presence. The apostle John wrote, "And I heard a loud voice from the throne, saying, 'Behold, the tabernacle of God is among men, and He will dwell among them, and they shall be His people, and God Himself will be among them, and He will wipe away every tear from their eyes; and there will no longer be any death; there will no longer be any mourning, or crying, or pain; the first things have passed away'" (Rev. 21:3–4 NASB).

Eternity is what we have to look forward to, but the questions most of us are asking are about life on this broken planet.

- How are we to live until then?
- Why does life have to be so hard?
- Why do the things of this world never really satisfy?
- Why are relationships so difficult and betrayal and loss so often our constant companions?

For those of you who relate to the never-ending search these questions bring about, there is good and bad news. The bad news first: you're not going to find satisfaction in this world. But the good news is, you can find it through intimacy with Jesus.

There is a longing in every heart to *know* God. Our Creator, who loves us, placed that desire within. Remember Ecclesiastes

3:11, which says that God has set "eternity" in our hearts (NIV)? That is why we are constantly searching and never satisfied. We know we were created for more than this world has to offer. This incessant longing for more drives me to my chair to meet with God every morning.

That longing began when I was in college. I started to seriously read the Bible. As I read, I realized my personal walk with God did not reflect the kind of relationship that the people recorded in Scripture experienced. I wanted to walk with Him and talk with Him. I didn't just want to know about God; I wanted to experience Him! First Corinthians 2:11–12 tells us that we have been given the Spirit of God, who knows the very thoughts of God. If His Spirit lives within me, why was I having such a difficult time knowing His will and discerning His voice?

> Why is it that we so often neglect the Word of God and only pray at mealtime or before bed? Could it be that we are living presumptuously?

This desire led me to commit time each day to Bible reading and prayer. Obviously there have been times in my life when I have been more disciplined than others, and every day is not a mountaintop experience. There are also seasons of life when it is more difficult to carve out this time. However, I soon came to realize that God's Word and prayer were nonnegotiable—absolute necessities. Without them the extraordinary Christian life is impossible!

Why is it that we so often neglect the Word of God and only pray at mealtime or before bed? Could it be that we are living presumptuously? Do we actually think we can make it in this broken world apart from God? How can we honestly believe we can live without being deceived, if Adam and Eve couldn't?

Prayer is our lifeline. It truly is to our spiritual bodies what breathing is to our physical bodies. Without it, our spiritual life will leave us gasping for more. It is absolutely imperative that you understand how much God desires to be in relationship with you.

This may be just the realization you need to step out in faith and turn your life over to Jesus in worship and prayer.

> Prayer is . . . to our spiritual bodies what breathing is to our physical bodies.

All of us are dissatisfied when we attempt to live our lives apart from a thriving relationship with God. This dissatisfaction can be traced all the way back to the garden. To understand the restlessness within us, we must go back to the beginning to comprehend all that was lost in the Fall. God created Adam and Eve and placed them in the perfect environment of the garden—lush vegetation, trees laden with fruit, rivers flowing with fresh water, no fear, no shame, no guilt (Gen. 1–2). It was an environment created specifically for relationship—the relationship between God and His people and between husband and wife. Adam and Eve enjoyed innocence, significance, and companionship. When God inspected His paradise, He was pleased and declared that it was excellent in every way.

But then something went drastically wrong. Suddenly, nothing seemed to satisfy. The perfect environment wasn't enough. The perfect spouse wasn't enough. It wasn't enough that God walked with Adam and Eve in the cool of the day. In fact, all it took was the hiss of the serpent and a vague promise of "something more" to cast doubt on God's Word and on His character. Eve fell for the lie that she was missing out (Gen. 3:1–7). She fell for it hook, line, and sinker, and Adam went right along with her.

In one split second, every negative emotion now known to humankind came crashing in. Instantly, Adam and Eve were overwhelmed by the shame, guilt, and fear that came along with their sin. Their futile attempt at fig-leaf clothes to hide their shame exposed their guilt. "Hiding. Covering up. Self-protection. Feeling exposed. They are telltale signs of shame."[2]

The next day, they heard the sound of the Lord God walking in the garden, and they hid from Him. Notice God's gentle approach. What did He do? He questioned them before He judged them. Genesis 3:9 says, "Then the LORD God called to the man, and said to him, 'Where are you?'" (NASB). Of course, God knew exactly where Adam was.

God knows all things, but He used that question to bring Adam to a realization, an understanding, of what had actually happened since he had chosen to rebel against God. God was really asking, *"Where are you now that you've gone your own way? Where are you now that you chose not to listen to Me, and you listened to the voice of the serpent? Where are you now, Adam? Where has your defiance taken you?"*

Like Adam and Eve, we, too, seek satisfaction outside of our relationship with God. We also listen to the voice of the enemy who taunts us with the suggestion that God is holding out on us—that we are missing out. Really? What had God been keeping from Adam and Eve—except pain, fear, guilt, shame, and death? What is God keeping from you except the same?

Adam answered God's "Where are you?" this way: "When I heard the sound of You coming in the garden, I was afraid because I am naked. So I hid *from You*." God probed deeper: "Who told you that you are naked? Have you eaten from the tree . . . I commanded you not to eat from?" (Gen. 3:10–11). As God's spotlight shone on his heart, Adam realized God knew exactly what he had done.

Imagine the humiliation Adam must have felt as the revelation of his sin echoed throughout the garden. Caught. Exposed. Ashamed. We all fear exposure of our sin before God. Sometimes that fear is what keeps us from praying and sends us into hiding as well. Yet, God would not leave them or us in hiding. He progressively asked Adam questions to reveal the real issue. Does God not do that with us? So often, when God is approaching us, convicting us, it is as though He is gently peeling back layers until we see the real root issue.

Adam's response sounds typical. He said, "It was the woman that You gave to be with me" (v. 12 NASB). Eve joined in the blame game with, "The serpent deceived me" (v. 13 NASB). What can we learn from them? We all want to pass the buck, don't we? We all want to blame somebody else. Adam hurled blame at Eve, and she hurled it at the serpent. Hiding and hurling are instinctive responses to guilt. They didn't want to be responsible for their own actions, and neither do we.

God immediately put a halt to the blame game. First, He said to the serpent, "Because you have done this, cursed are you more than all cattle, and more than every beast of the field; on your belly you will go, and dust you will eat all the days of your life; and I will put enmity between you and the woman, and between your seed and her seed; he shall bruise you on the head, and you shall bruise him on the heel" (Gen. 3:14–15 NASB).

This passage is the first time the "Promised One" is mentioned in God's Word. God's way back to Him would be through His Son, born of the seed of woman. In the midst of the curse, there is a ray of hope—the Promised One would crush the serpent's head!

God then pronounced judgment on Adam and Eve. He told Eve that her pain in childbirth would be greatly increased and that she would experience conflict and separation in her relationship with her husband. Gone were the days of innocence and trust. Now their relationship would be a struggle, the result of sin.

Wives, we need to listen cautiously to God's words to Adam. He told him because he had *listened to his wife*, the ground would be cursed. Toil and pain became a part of their daily reality. How careful we must be as we influence our husbands with our words. Most of us have not considered how influential we really are. We will each give an account for every word we speak (Matt. 12:36). May we wield this influence prayerfully and carefully.

From the beginning, God's great mercy has been evident. God pronounced judgment, but then after the judgment, He protected Adam and Eve. He took care of them. He provided for them. God took an animal He declared good and killed it, establishing from the beginning that it takes the shedding of innocent blood to cover sin. With the skins, He created clothes for Adam and Eve, for they could no longer walk about uncovered.

God banished Adam and Eve from the garden, protecting them from themselves. He prevented them from eating from the Tree of Life and being forever separated from God in their sinful condition: "After driving them out, He stationed winged guardians at

> How careful we must be as we influence our husbands with our words. . . . We will each give an account for every word we speak.

the east end of the garden of Eden and set up a sword of flames which . . . turned back and forth to guard the way to the tree of life" (Gen. 3:24). Why? Because God still desired to dwell with Adam and Eve and with us. He values relationships over rules.

But breaking the rules separates us from God and from one another, distorting our relationships. The rules are in place to protect us and to point us to the Father.

With God, mercy triumphs over judgment—if you doubt that, read the book of Judges. Relationship is always the priority. Rules guard the relationship, which is at the center of the heart of God. God yearns for us and longs for us to be restored to right relationship with Him.

To read more in God's autobiography about the garden and the Fall, read Genesis 1–3.

QUESTIONS TO CONSIDER

1. Reflect on what you have read. Conflict is inevitable. How has conflict in relationships affected you? How has it affected your marriage?

   Conflict will either drive us to despair or to our chair. We will face up when we go facedown.

2. Is there any sin in your life that continues to separate you from God? Have you brought it to the Lord? Let His Spirit "peel back" your defenses and get to the root of the issue.

3. God has pronounced and yet He has provided. In the midst of it all, He gives a promise—He will make a way. He will not leave Adam and Eve. He will not leave us. What promise of God brings you great hope and comfort?

NOTES

CHAPTER TWO

THE GOD OF THE COVENANT

GOD CHOOSES A PEOPLE

Remember you are people who have been set apart for Him; He has chosen you to be His own possession out of all the peoples on the earth.

–Deuteronomy 14:2

To fully grasp the significance of the tabernacle and its link to our prayer life, we will trace God's desire for relationship with humankind through Scripture. Tracing God's hand through all of the details of His pursuit of and provision for man is a convincing proof of His existence and character.

Generations passed, and life outside the garden became routine. Sin increased, and some may have wondered if God would fulfill His promise to send the One who would break sin's curse.

God had spoken, and He always fulfills His Word. But His timing is not ours, nor are His ways (Isa. 55:8–9).

In an unpredictable move only God would make, He chose a seventy-five-year-old, childless idol worshiper (Josh. 24:2) named Abram (God later changed his name to Abraham) and called on him to leave everything. To this unlikely man God said these astounding words: "Out of you I will make a great nation, and all people on the earth will be blessed through you. Deliverance is on its way. Follow Me and I will bless you." Then Abram, a tent dweller, packed it all up and followed God from Haran to the place that God would show him.

After this sovereign call, Abram began a practice of worship. He built several altars during his journey. There he would call on the name of the Lord.

We, too, need to have a practice of worship as well as a special place or places where we call on the Lord. These places become sacred to us. Do you have a habit and a place of worship? As Oswald Chambers said, "Any soul who has not that solitary place alone with God is in supreme peril spiritually."[1]

For me, that place is a chair in our great room. Beside my chair I have a basket that contains all the things I need for my time with the Lord. I don't want to waste valuable time searching for my Bible or a pen. I want my place to be prepared. But back to our story.

God led Abram to Canaan and appeared to him one starlit night. He invited Abram to come outside and gaze up at the stars. He said, "Number the stars if you are able—Abram, yes, you, advanced in age and childless. Your descendants will outnumber the stars." Against all evidence to the contrary, Abram believed, and God "reckoned," or "credited," it to him as righteousness

(Gen. 15:6 NASB; NIV). Charles Ryrie notes that to credit Abraham as righteous was "a judicial verdict whereby God said of Abraham 'not guilty!'"[2]

I have been to Israel, and I have always been amazed by the sky at night. Looking up, there seems to be no limit to the stars. God says to those of us who are "in Christ" that all of the promises of God are yes in Christ Jesus. We have been grafted into the very lineage of Abraham, and thus there are no limits to what God can do and what He desires to do through you! If you are "in Christ," then you are one of those stars Abram believed God for. You are a descendant of Abraham.

From the very beginning, faith in God and His Word have been the requirements for salvation. That's how we are reckoned, or counted, righteous. When we believe, and call upon the name of the Lord, His righteousness is credited to us (2 Cor. 5:21). As a result, our sin account is marked, "PAID IN FULL"!

Belief leads to further revelation. After Abram's conversation with God, God caused a deep sleep to come over Abram, and He took him into His confidence. God let him know that his descendants were going to be in Egypt for four hundred years. They were going to be oppressed, but God was going to raise up a deliverer who would then bring them back to this land of promise that God had told Abraham his descendants would possess. Not only would they be delivered, but they would come out of Egypt with many possessions (Gen. 15:14). That night, God foreshadowed His plan to provide for the tabernacle. The provision was in place.

> There are no limits to what God can do and what He desires to do through you!

God had Abram bring five specific animals (a three-year-old heifer, a three-year-old female goat, a three-year-old ram, a turtledove, and a pigeon) and cut them in two, except for the birds. Through the cutting of a covenant with Abram, God obligated Himself to fulfill the promise He had made. This was a common practice in that day. Usually both parties would pass between the animal parts, declaring that death should occur to them if they broke the covenant. This time, God alone passed between the animal parts, revealed as a smoking oven and a flaming torch, while Abram did nothing. God would birth a nation through Abram. Thus, God chose a people. Through His chosen people, He would send the ultimate deliverer, His Son.

God does not need our help, but He does desire our cooperation.

At the time God called him, Abram was not capable of possessing the land. He was the head of one little family and he didn't even have an heir. Abram was powerless to accomplish all that God had spoken. One of the primary lessons we learn from Abram is the importance of taking God at His Word. God promised and Abram believed. "By faith he journeyed to the land of the promise as a foreigner; he lived in tents, as did Isaac and Jacob, his fellow heirs to the promise because Abraham looked ahead to a city with foundations, a city laid out and built by God" (Heb. 11:9–10).

God is always faithful to His Word. If He has spoken, He will fulfill it. But He doesn't always operate in our time frame. Abram was seventy-five when God called him. There would be twenty-five long years of waiting and trying to help God out, as well as a name change, before God would send the promised heir—Isaac. Abram, now Abraham, was one hundred when Isaac was born.

The thought of this centenarian changing diapers leads us to a second observation. God does not need our help, but He does desire our cooperation. Our job is to believe and obey. God will fulfill His promise in His way and in His timing—even if it means granting a promised heir to a hundred-year-old man and his ninety-year-old wife. They waited two and a half decades for the promise to be fulfilled, from the time of the covenant until Abraham actually received an heir. I have a friend who calls this "gap time." What we do in the "gap time" is so important. So often during this time God is pruning and preparing us for His promise.

Can you think about a time in your own life when God spoke to you through His Word, and yet it may have been years before the promise came to fruition? Maybe you have a specific prayer request for which you believe God has given you a promise, but you haven't yet seen it fulfilled. It is so important that we trust God's Word and don't give up. Continue to pray that promise back to God until He makes it a reality.

I sensed God calling me to the ministry when I was twelve. I remember being in a worship service and having an overwhelming sense of God's presence. I knew inwardly that God was calling me to surrender my future and commit to follow Him, much as Abraham did. At that moment, like no other moment before, I was aware that my life was not my own. I responded with a verbal "yes" as I walked forward during the invitation and told my pastor I felt called to full-time Christian service—whatever that might mean.

I met my husband in college, and we both believed the Lord had brought us together to be life partners in ministry. The only issue was, I thought I had been called to missions. After much soul-searching and prayer, I was convinced that the Lord had called me to be Steve's wife, and that meant I would be a pastor's wife.

Have you ever thought that you "missed God"? It may be that you haven't missed Him but just missed His timing. It would be thirty years after that initial call before God would renew the call to missions. At that time in my life, I was taking part in a video-driven Bible study. The teacher, Beth Moore, was talking about a mission trip to India, and at that moment, I sensed the Holy Spirit saying, *"The time is now. I am calling you to take the gospel to women of other nations."*

Nothing curtails materialism and self-absorption like . . . ministering to those who have nothing by the world's standards.

Immediately my mind began to race and wonder how He was going to work this out. Two weeks later, as I was walking out of a Sunday school class, I was approached by one of our businessmen who had a ministry in Romania. He said he had been praying for several years, asking the Lord to provide a group of women to go to Romania and do women's conferences. He asked if I would pray about going. I said, "Ronnie, I don't have to pray; God has already called me." For once, I had not rushed ahead and tried to help God out. I had been praying and wondering how the Lord would bring it about, and now He was showing me.

Less than a year later, twenty-three of us went to Romania and conducted three women's conferences. God knit our hearts with the hearts of the women who knew firsthand what it was like to experience religious persecution under a Communist regime. We were sisters in Christ, and we became friends almost instantly. We realized how much we had in common as women, wives, and mothers, regardless of our different languages and backgrounds.

A decade after the overthrow of Communism, they were able to freely gather and worship the Lord and learn more about Him through His Word. Their stories of faith under former Communist oppression made me feel unworthy to be teaching them. My life was enriched and challenged by their courage and faith in the midst of such intense persecution.

Since that first trip, the Lord has given me the privilege of going to several other countries to share the gospel and teach His Word. All four of our children have been able to go on foreign mission trips as well. In fact, I would highly recommend mission trips for your family or for your children with their youth group. Nothing curtails materialism and self-absorption like spending time in a third-world country and ministering to those who have nothing by the world's standards and yet possess such joy and purpose in Christ.

The call to missions had been a genuine call from the Lord. His timing was and is perfect. My responsibility continues to be to believe and obey. What do we miss when we haven't learned to discern His voice? It is through daily seeking Him that He reveals Himself and His will.

I am not to worry about tomorrow (Matt. 6:34) but to focus on today. God grants just enough light for me to take the next step. I can't expect further revelation until I am walking obediently in what He has already revealed. Are you walking obediently with Him today?

As Oswald Chambers so rightly said, "Faith never knows where it is being led, but it loves and knows the One who is leading."[3]

QUESTIONS TO CONSIDER

1. What promise has God given you that you have not yet seen ful-filled? Allow Him to renew your faith, as you trust Him for His perfect timing.

2. God always keeps His promises. We see in the life of Abraham how God chose a people through which He would send the prom-ised "seed" of woman (Gen. 3:15 KJV). As followers of Christ, we, too, should be promise keepers. Reflect on the importance of being a person of your word.

NOTES

CHAPTER THREE

GOD CHOOSES A DELIVERER

*The Eternal spoke with Moses
face-to-face, just as a friend
speaks to another friend.*

—Exodus 33:11

God fulfilled the vision He had given Abraham through Isaac, Jacob (whose name was changed to Israel), and Joseph. Through Joseph God moved the Israelites to Egypt where they lived 400 years. They multiplied and became as numerous as "the stars" (Gen. 15:5).

But then a new pharaoh came to power who didn't know Joseph or respect the God of the Israelites. Feeling threatened by these people who were multiplying so rapidly, he made them slaves and began to oppress them through taskmasters. This didn't slow down the growth of the Israelites, so he commanded that their baby boys be thrown into the Nile (Ex. 1:22).

At this time, the people cried out to God, and He sent a newborn—Moses—to be their deliverer. Because of the pharaoh's mandate that all Hebrew baby boys should be killed, Moses' mother hid him for three months after he was born. At that point, fearing his discovery, she made a little ark and placed him among the reeds along the edge of the Nile. One day, the daughter of Pharaoh came down to bathe in the Nile and discovered him. God moved her heart with compassion, and she took Moses as her own.

Thus, God sovereignly protected and prepared His deliverer.

At age forty, Moses thought he could deliver his people his own way. But after killing an Egyptian who was mistreating an Israelite, Moses was forced to flee for his life. He spent the next forty years in the desert.

Moses thought he was beyond being used. But God was not finished with him. God appeared to him in a bush that was on fire, and yet was not consumed (Ex. 3:2). From this fire, the Lord called Moses to deliver His people from Egypt. After many excuses, Moses headed for Egypt, accompanied by his brother, Aaron. God had promised to be with Moses and to perform many miraculous signs through him. God instructed Moses to tell Pharaoh, "Let my son go, so he can worship me" (Ex. 4:23 NLT). Pharaoh refused, hardening his heart.

> God would teach the Israelites that their protection from death came from the blood of a lamb.

God is faithful to His Word. He sent ten plagues upon the Egyptians and their gods, and in the end, Pharaoh let the Israelites go. It would be through the tenth plague that God would teach the Israelites that their protection from death came from the blood of a lamb. The death angel, sent to bring God's judgment upon the Egyptians by killing the firstborn in every home, "passed over" the

Israelite homes because death had already taken place there. The blood of the sacrificed lambs—one for each household—that they placed on their doors protected their firstborn. When the angel saw the blood, he moved on to the next house.

The blood of the Passover lambs foreshadowed *the* Lamb (Jesus), who would come as a sacrifice and shed His blood—once for all—for all of humankind. When His blood is applied to our lives at salvation, we will not experience the second death (Rev. 21)—the lake of fire.

The Israelites didn't leave Egypt until they had followed God's directives and plundered the Egyptians, taking with them articles of silver, articles of gold, and clothing. God had them ask for all that they would need for what He was yet to reveal. God was providing beforehand the materials He would require to build the tabernacle.

After the Israelites had left Egypt and been rescued by God through the Red Sea, God led them by the pillar of fire and cloud to Mount Sinai. Here He said to His rescued people, "Now if you will *hear My voice,* obey what I say, and keep My covenant, then you—out of all the nations of the world—will be My treasured people. After all, the earth belongs to Me. You will be My kingdom of priests, a nation holy *and set apart*" (Ex. 19:5–6). God brought them out of slavery to establish a relationship with them. The relationship always precedes revelation.

Sacrifices were offered and the blood was sprinkled on the people so that their sins were covered. The people confessed that they would be obedient to all that God had commanded. After Moses had consecrated the people, the Lord invited Moses and the elders to come up on the mountain. "Then Moses took Aaron, Nadab,

Abihu, and 70 of Israel's elders and went up *the mountain*. There they saw Israel's God" (Ex. 24:9–10).

In Exodus 24, the Bible gives us a glimpse of the threshold of the throne room. Every time heaven is described in Scripture, it is the same vivid description. Heaven is grand and glorious and so difficult to describe—you will read phrases such as "it looked like," "it had the appearance of," and "it was something like." Why do those who have seen heaven stumble trying to describe it? Because no one has the vocabulary to express what they have seen and experienced in the presence of God.

What did they see? We know no man can see God's face. No man has ever seen His face, Scripture tells us, because it would kill us. The full blaze of His holiness would destroy us. But Moses and the elders were able to see a form of God. "Beneath His feet, there appeared to be paving stones of sapphire, as *pure and* clear as the sky above. But God did not raise His hand against the leaders of Israel *to strike them down*. They beheld the True God, and they feasted and drank *in His presence*" (Ex. 24:10–11).

In the midst of this experience, God called Moses to come farther up on the mountain, and Joshua went with him. Then God called Moses on farther still, and "Moses made his way up the mountain" (Ex. 24:15).

In Exodus 24:15–18, the manifest presence of God was depicted by fire and smoke with flashes of lightning and thunder:

> A *thick* cloud blanketed the mountain because the Eternal's glory had settled upon it. The cloud stayed there for six days; and when the seventh day arrived, the Eternal spoke to Moses from the cloud. For the Israelites below, the Eternal's glory appeared to be a consuming fire on the top of the mountain. As Moses walked further toward the top, he was swallowed by the

cloud *of God's glory,* and he remained there for *a total of* 40 days and 40 nights.

How did God reveal His presence to the Israelites? How did they know when He was near? They all saw the cloud and the fire. The purpose of the cloud was to cover. It protected Israel from the full blaze of God's glory, of His holiness. And the fire appeared to consume. It was purifying, because He is holy. God granted them this picture of His presence through the fire and the cloud. The whole mountain appeared to be consumed with it.

And the Lord would later say, in Numbers 12:8, "And with him [Moses] I communicate face-to-face. We speak directly and without riddles. He can even see the very form of the Eternal." That is how Moses experienced the presence of God. The people saw the cloud and fire and heard the voice of the Lord. Thus, they trusted Moses when he spoke for the Lord (Ex. 19:9).

> God's desire from the beginning was to rescue us from ourselves. This rescue was not for our relief but for relationship.

God is preparing the people before He gives them instructions for the tabernacle, a place where He can literally dwell among them and not consume them. A place where He can be approached so that He can instruct His people, a place where He can spend time with them, a place of safety. That is how tender His mercies are toward us. God longs to be with us. He desires to be able to lead us, to guide us, to be in the midst of us, and yet He must protect us from the unveiled force of His holiness.

God's desire from the beginning was to rescue us from ourselves. This rescue was not for our relief but for relationship. God spoke to Adam and Eve. God spoke to Abraham. God spoke to Moses. God still speaks. He speaks primarily through His Word, but He also speaks to us through His Spirit, who lives within us if we are believers. As your relationship grows, you learn to discern His voice. He said in John 10:4 that His sheep follow Him because they know His voice.

We must spend time with someone to really get to know him or her. When people I know well call me on the phone, they don't have to identify themselves; I know their voices. When my children would call out to me at home, I recognized their voices even if I couldn't see them.

Spend time with Jesus so you can discern His voice. He still speaks, and as my husband likes to say, "It's not audible; it's louder than that." Are you listening?

QUESTIONS TO CONSIDER

1. When is the last time God spoke to you through His Word? What verse or verses did He use?

2. What are you currently praying about and waiting for God to answer?

CHAPTER FOUR

GOD'S DWELLING

THE TABERNACLE

"I will **meet** with you there. I will **speak**
to you from above the seat of mercy
between the two winged creatures
that sit atop the covenant chest.
From there, I will speak to you about
all the commands *and instructions*
I have for the people of Israel."

–Exodus 25:22

God gave Moses His commands for the people when he was on the mountain. God's people were to be set apart from the other nations. Different. Distinct. Unique. They were not to worship the pagan gods of the other countries; they were to worship the one true God. Thus, God gave them commands to be obeyed. He demanded an exclusive relationship with them. As my friend Joni Shankles so beautifully stated, "Intimate relationships are exclusive by nature. Choosing to be intimate with God means you are excluding other things, other people, and other pursuits."

God set His people apart through His relationship with them. He also gave them commands to be followed and then gave them the design for His dwelling among them—the tabernacle. Along with the commands came blessings for obedience and curses for disobedience (Deut. 28–30). God demanded obedience from the heart—the place of intimate relationship.

> The tabernacle was not just a place for God to dwell. It was a place of worship that was based on relationship.

It is interesting to note that God gave the people only ten commandments, but chapter after chapter of instructions for His dwelling and how His people were to live with Him in their midst. The tabernacle was not just a place for God to dwell. It was a place of worship that was based on relationship.

God had ordered the Israelites, who were packing up and preparing to depart from Egypt, to ask their Egyptian neighbors for "articles of silver and articles of gold, and clothing; and the LORD had given the people favor in the sight of the Egyptians, so that they let them have their request. Thus they plundered the Egyptians" (Ex. 12:35–36 NASB). The Lord commanded them to ask of the Egyptians the very things that He would later require. The Israelites obeyed, even though they didn't understand. I am certain they may have thought this plunder was, in effect, payment for their enslavement. Yet, God had a higher purpose for its use.

God's plan for the gold and silver was given to Moses in extensive detail. As Dr. Olford, author of *The Tabernacle: Camping with God*, noted: "It is most remarkable to discover that no less than fifty chapters in the Old and New Testaments are devoted to the construction, ritual and priesthood of the Tabernacle and the meaning of them all."[1] In the book of Hebrews, from the King James Version, we are told that the tabernacle and the priesthood were the "shadow of heavenly things" (8:5) and "the figures of the true" (9:24). Thus, God was very specific about His instructions and the command to follow exactly what He instructed in creating the tabernacle and its articles.

When the time came for constructing the tabernacle, "all the Israelites, both men and women, who felt moved to provide the material needed to do this work, brought these offerings willingly and set them before the Eternal One exactly as He had instructed Moses" (Ex. 35:29). Then God selected men and filled them with His Spirit to enable them to have the skill needed to perform the work of an engraver and designer for the articles.

God told Moses to be sure to do exactly what He had *shown* him on the mountain. In his book *The Way into the Holiest,* F. B. Meyer notes the significance of the revelation on the mountain:

> But, in addition to the minute description thus given, there appears to have been presented to the mind of Moses some representation of the things which he was bidden to construct. It was as if the eternal realities which had dwelt forever in the mind of God took some visible shape before his vision. The unseen became visible. The eternal took form. A pattern was shown him. He trod the aisles of the true Tabernacle. He beheld the heavenly things themselves. And it was after this pattern that he was repeatedly urged and commanded to build.[2]

If we look for it, we can see a foreshadowing of the cross of Christ in the design and placement of the articles of the tabernacle. The tabernacle was divided into three parts: the outer court, and the inner court, which was divided into two—the Holy Place and the Holy of Holies. The Holy of Holies was the innermost section, where God's presence dwelled.

We know from the New Testament that our bodies are temples of the Lord. We, too, are divided into three parts—spirit, soul, and body (1 Thess. 5:23). God's presence through His Holy Spirit dwells in the innermost part of our being—our spirit.

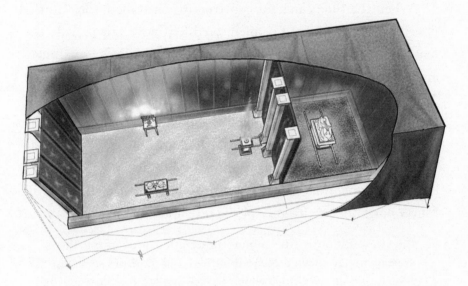

As we work our way through the tabernacle, we will discover how each part not only points to a heavenly reality, but also depicts and points to Christ. "Christ is the *perfect Tabernacle*. In Him is fulfilled all that the Tabernacle in the wilderness typified and prefigured."[3]

Just as the priests prepared themselves to enter the presence of the Lord, we should prepare *ourselves* before entering His presence. Before we pray, we should prepare our hearts. Prayer is such a miracle! That the Creator of the universe desires to commune with us is a concept almost too good to be true. And yet, we see in Scripture God's desire to commune with and be known by His people. How can we, who on this side of the cross have been invited in, not take advantage of this great opportunity and privilege?

My favorite woman in the New Testament is Mary of Bethany. She is seen only three times in Scripture, but all three times she is at Jesus' feet. In the first encounter with her, in Luke 10, the Lord defends her when her sister, Martha, rebukes her.

Martha was frustrated that she had been left in the kitchen to do all the work by herself. Mary was sitting with the disciples at the feet of Jesus, listening to Him teach. Jesus told Martha she was anxious and concerned about so many things, "but only one thing is necessary, for Mary has chosen the good part, which shall not be taken away from her" (Luke 10:42 NASB).

The "one thing" Mary had chosen was time with Jesus. When I make my time with Christ the priority of my day, I am choosing the "one thing" that Christ commends. When Christ through His Spirit speaks to me and reveals truth through His Word, I am changed. Not only am I changed, but the truth He has revealed can never be taken away from me.

The last time we see Mary with Christ, He is having a meal in the home of Simon (John 12:1–11; Mark 14:3–9). Mary, who was also present at the meal, did something unexpected and very extravagant. She took a vial of perfume worth a year's wages and anointed Jesus for burial. How did she know? No one else did. Mary had chosen and Christ had revealed. He still reveals Himself to those who choose.

Being with Christ is the "one thing" that must be chosen. It is an act of the will but also a decision that must be fought for. When you set aside time to be with Christ in His Word and in prayer, the enemy will put up a fight. As the great man of prayer Samuel Chadwick stated, "The one concern of the devil is to keep the saints from praying. He fears nothing from prayerless studies, prayerless work, prayerless religion. He laughs at our toil, mocks at our wisdom, but trembles when we pray."[4]

The truths you hear when someone speaks, or even when you read a book, are often forgotten. But when God speaks to you, that truth becomes a part of you and you will not forget it. Revealed truth changes the way you think and conforms you to the image of Christ.

QUESTIONS TO CONSIDER

1. Jesus said that He would send the Holy Spirit, who would teach us everything we need to know (John 14:26). Are you allowing Him to teach you as you read God's Word?

2. What has God been teaching you? What new truth has He revealed?

NOTES

PART TWO

THE ARTICLES OF THE TABERNACLE

A FORESHADOWING OF CHRIST

The tabernacle may be best understood as a picture of what actually exists in the presence of God. But it is also a signpost pointing to Jesus Christ, who would be its fulfillment. Jesus is the presence of God among us—Immanuel—God with us!

Jesus Christ was God in the flesh, the very embodiment of God the Father. For truly, in Him, "all the fullness of Deity dwells in bodily form" (Col. 2:9 NASB). John stated in John 1:18, "No one has seen God at any time; the only begotten God who is in the bosom of the Father, He has explained Him" (NASB). Jesus walked among us as our model for living and our picture of God. The Lion of Judah is also the Lamb of God slain before the foundation of the world. He was the sacrifice made once for all.

CHAPTER FIVE

THE GATE
(EXODUS 27:9–19)

"I am the gate; whoever enters
through me will be saved."

–John 10:9 (NIV)

There was only one gate or entrance to the courtyard. The
priests were to enter dressed in the garments prescribed by God
and prepared for their position and service. God demonstrated
through this gate that there is one way to God, and we must come
as He requires.

Scripture is very clear that God's desire from the beginning has been to restore relationship with those He created. He did this through His Son. Our rebellious nature screams against a sovereign God who speaks through His Word and declares what is right and true. Mark Thompson notes:

> It was as unfashionable in the first century to proclaim Jesus as the Son of the living God, the only one who can save men and women, as it is in the twenty-first. People were offended then too, social structures were disrupted, violence was not an uncommon repercussion of making the claim. Furthermore, the unambiguous testimony of Scripture in this regard is the engine room of Christian missions, which is fuelled by love rather than fear or a desire to extinguish difference . . . Any demand that the call to come to Jesus be silenced or modified so as not to offend those who already have other commitments can only have one ultimate origin.[1]

Jesus said of Himself, "I am the way, and the truth, and the life; no one comes to the Father but through Me" (John 14:6 NASB). In addition, He described Himself as the gate of the sheep. In John 10:9 He said, "I am the gate; whoever enters through me will be saved. They will come in and go out, and find pasture" (NIV).

God's requirement is clear: we enter through Christ. When we come to Christ, He clothes us with His righteousness and we are invited into the very presence of God. We do not come on our own merit but through the perfect sacrifice of our substitute. As conference speaker Betty Vick notes, "You never find, in all of Scripture, the priest examining the sinner [the Israelite] who brought the offering. The priest only examined the sacrifice to make sure that it was without spot or blemish. Praise His holy name that is also true today."[2] Thus, the worst sinner can come to God through Jesus, our spotless sacrifice, and be made clean!

Without Christ's sinless life, death, and bodily resurrection, there would be no hope for humankind. You and I would be lost without any hope of a right relationship with God. All of the Old Testament laws reveal our inability to be "good enough" to enter God's presence. God's law demanded perfection, and we all fall short (Rom. 3:23).

Christ conquered death, hell, and the grave and came out with the keys (Rev. 1:18). He died in our place and paid our debt. It is only through Christ that we enter into relationship with God. There is no other way, regardless of how sincere we may be.

I recently accompanied my husband on a flight to New York. We boarded the plane and heard the flight attendant announce that the plane was headed to LaGuardia, and if that was not your final destination, you needed to deplane. If someone on the plane had sincerely desired to go to San Francisco, that flier's sincerity would not have affected his or her destination. You must be on the right plane.

Other religions tell people how they can work their way to heaven. They may be sincere. But if they are not entering through Christ, they will be sincerely wrong. Their destination will not be heaven. They are on the broad path that leads to destruction. Jesus said:

> "*There are two paths before you; you may take only one path.* One doorway is narrow. *And one door is wide.* Go through the narrow door. For the wide door leads to a wide path, and the wide path is broad; the wide, broad path is easy, and the wide, broad, easy path has many, many people on it; but the wide, broad, easy, crowded path leads to death. Now then that narrow door leads to a narrow road that in turn leads to life. It is hard to find that road. Not many people manage it." (Matt. 7:13–14)

Brennan Manning said, "The gate that is truly narrow but accessible to all is that of humility. The narrow way, the narrow gate, is for those who become like little children again. 'Whoever humbles himself like this child is the greatest in the kingdom of heaven.'"[3]

We now have six grandchildren. Our granddaughter who is five is the oldest. Our son and his wife live about an hour away from us, which makes it possible for us to see them fairly frequently. I am often struck by my granddaughter's innocence and the sheer joy of living that she exudes. When I see her, she runs to me, jumps up in my arms, and gives me what we call a double hug. She wraps her arms and legs around me and squeals with delight.

There are times I want to freeze the moment. With all my heart, I want to protect her innocence and wonder. It is at those moments that I am reminded that the Father said we are to become like children if we want to enter the kingdom of heaven. It is that childlike trust and joy that thrills the heart of the Father, just as my granddaughter's childish enthusiasm thrills mine.

As Christians, we should, of all people, be full of hope and joy. For all of Scripture points to God's desire to redeem His people and indwell them through His Spirit. Could we ever hear any better news? He came to rescue us. There is a way out of brokenness and into His peace and joy. There is a "happily ever after" being prepared for us. But we must, in childlike faith, believe.

One of the most beautiful and graphic pictures of this good news is the tabernacle and its articles. Let's begin our walk through the tabernacle and glean from it the truths revealed in this model for worship.

We enter into relationship with God through His Son and our substitutionary sacrifice—Jesus Christ. As we cross the threshold through Christ, there is a life exchange—our life for His. This is salvation.

 QUESTIONS TO CONSIDER

**Recall your salvation. I encourage you to write out your salvation story.**

1. What was your life like before Christ?

2. How did you meet Christ?

3. How has Christ changed your life?

NOTES

CHAPTER SIX

THE BRAZEN ALTAR

(EXODUS 27:1-8)

Therefore I urge you, brethren, by the
mercies of God, to present your bodies a
living and holy sacrifice, acceptable to God,
which is your spiritual service of worship.

–Romans 12:1 (NASB)

Once we enter through the gate into the courtyard, we encounter the brazen altar. It is here that we must lay down our old life and our rebellious will.

The altar was square and made of acacia wood, covered in bronze. The metal created a fireproof covering. "Only comparatively recently have scientists discovered what an ingenious, fire-resisting invention is hard wood overlaid with copper and hermetically sealed. How wonderfully this combination speaks of the Person of our Lord Jesus Christ, who endured the fires of Calvary without being consumed; like the bush that Moses saw in the wilderness which burned with fire but was not destroyed"[1] There was a horn on each corner of the brazen altar and a grate beneath. There were rings on each corner for the poles that were used when transporting the altar. The fire on this altar never went out. Here the priests offered the burnt offering, the grain offering, the peace offering, the sin offering, and the guilt offering (Lev. 1–5). The altar is a foreshadowing of the cross and the once-for-all sacrifice that Christ would make of Himself. Christ alone fulfilled the sacrifices required by God, and through His death and resurrection we can be born again.

Christ offers the gift of eternal life to all who will repent and believe. When we die to our flesh, we are made alive in the Spirit. Christ must be Lord of our lives. We no longer belong to ourselves, but now belong to and represent Him.

A corpse has no feelings, rights, or the ability to be offended. Paul wrote, "I have been crucified with Christ; and it is no longer I who live, but Christ lives in me" (Gal. 2:20 NASB). Is Christ really living in and through me? If for me "to live is Christ" (Phil. 1:21 NASB), then I will be more alive to what He thinks of me than what anyone else thinks of me. I will stand before my Lord one day, and I desire with all of my heart to hear Him say I accomplished His purpose for my life.

Martin Luther said, "God creates out of nothing. Therefore until a man is nothing God can make nothing out of him."[2] We must come to the end of ourselves, leaving all on the altar. Romans 12:1 tells us we are to present our bodies to the Lord as a living sacrifice. This sacrifice is a burnt offering, with nothing left over, and the entire offering consumed.

As Nancy Leigh DeMoss accurately stated in her book *Surrender*:

> The person who has never acknowledged Christ's right to rule over his life has no basis for assurance of salvation. He may claim to be a Christian; he may have walked an aisle or prayed the sinner's prayer; he may know how to speak "Christianese"; he may be heavily involved in Christian activities; but if he thinks he can have a relationship with God by retaining control over his life and somehow trying to fit Jesus in with everything else, he is deceived and is still at war with God.[3]

After becoming a pastor's wife, a strange thing happened to me. I lost the ability to speak in front of adults. I was an elementary education major with a master's degree in special education. I loved children and decided that I was just more comfortable with them. This became my excuse when asked to do anything in front of adults. If you have walked with the Lord very long, you know that He will not leave you in your comfort zone, and He doesn't allow excuses.

The Lord began to impress upon me that I should not be bound by fear. I started to realize how irrational my fear really was. But no matter how hard I tried, every time I read Scripture or spoke in a group of adults, I had something akin to a panic attack. I could feel my heart pounding in my chest and my ears, and my breathing became shallow and rapid. Obviously this was embarrassing and only served to increase the symptoms.

When we moved to our second church, I became active in a ministers' wives organization. I never volunteered for anything other than service projects. But one day the organization's leader asked me if I would do the devotional for the next month. My immediate response was to say no, but I sensed the Lord telling me this was an opportunity to face my fear and trust Him. So I said yes and began praying and preparing.

I prepared the devotional. I wrote it out on five-by-seven-inch cards and practically had it memorized. I decided that if Paul could be a fool for Christ, I could too. And that was exactly what I expected to be.

The time came for the monthly meeting, and I stood to share what I believed the Lord had given me. Before I opened my mouth, my heart was pounding and I was experiencing shortness of breath. I managed to get through the devotion and sit down. I was so relieved it was over, and breathed in prayer to the Lord, "If anybody got anything out of that, it will be a miracle of the Holy Spirit!"

The women were kind, and I left that day thinking I would never be asked to do that again. Yet, in a couple of days, another pastor's wife called to tell me how blessed she had been by the devotional, and she wanted to know if I would be the speaker for their retreat. I don't know if you have ever experienced your mouth taking off before your brain was engaged, but that is exactly what happened. I began to tell her that I just didn't do that sort of thing, but I had a friend who was called into women's ministry, and I would be happy to ask her if she was available.

I quickly got off the phone and slumped against the wall. At that moment, it was as if the Lord said, *"I thought you said the answer would be yes to anything I asked of you."* I replied, "But—but, Lord, I'm not eloquent . . . I am just really not good at that sort of thing."

I knew immediately God was not going to let me off the hook. Then it hit me! I could ask my friend Debbie to do the retreat with me. That way, if I passed out or had a heart attack, she could just keep right on teaching, and the ladies wouldn't miss a thing.

> I knew in my head that God was able to do anything; I just wasn't convinced He could do it with me.

Feeling proud of myself, I called my friend. She was available and thought it would be great fun to do it together. I then called the pastor's wife and told her she was getting two for the price of one— just pay Debbie, I told her. Still feeling a bit smug, I told my husband about my solution when he came in from church that afternoon. Without missing a beat, he said, "So, Moses, you need an Aaron?"

"Oh Lord, was that really what I was doing?" Taking my struggle to the Lord in prayer, I realized my lack of faith in Him. I also realized my desire for comfort and how I had schemed to make things happen according to my plan. What had God told Moses when he began making excuses about his inability to speak? The Lord asked him, "Who is it that gives a person a mouth? Who determines whether one person speaks and another doesn't?" (Ex. 4:11). I knew in my head that God was able to do anything; I just wasn't convinced He could do it with me.

Ever been there? In times like this, we must go to the altar and lay down whatever is holding us back. Nail it to the cross. I didn't overcome my fear of speaking to adults overnight, but that was the beginning of facing my fear and trusting God. There were many more trips to the altar. As I continued to obey, He continued to loose the noose of fear. Fear is like a noose, you know. It threatens to choke the life out of you!

And oh, what I would have missed if I hadn't obeyed. I would still be in the clutches of fear, unable to experience the joy of teaching God's Word to women and watching as their lives are transformed. Now I can share my story with others to encourage them to take whatever is holding them back to the altar. It was at the altar that the Lord revealed the "root" of my fear. It seems so obvious now, but at the time I was totally unaware. The root was pride. I cared more about what the people listening to me thought about me than I did what my Lord thought about me.

> Most of us fear losing control—which is an absolute absurdity. We actually control nothing!

I cringe now when I think about it and wonder how I could have been so clueless! Yet, God is patient and long-suffering. He continues to peel back the layers of my flesh, exposing where I depend upon myself. Self-reliance leads to sin that must be renounced and laid on the altar. It is only after our flesh is crucified that we experience resurrection life—the abundant life that Christ died to purchase.

Why do so many of us settle for so much less? I think most of us fear losing control—which is an absolute absurdity. We actually control nothing! All that we seek to control is out of our hands, but it is not beyond the reach of our Father. We must take our concerns to Him in prayer and then trust Him to work on our behalf.

Manley Beasley was a great man of faith whose teaching significantly impacted my life. He once said, "Faith is reason at rest with God."[4] I cannot reason my way into rest and peace. God's prescription for peace is prayer with thanksgiving. As I turn my anxious thoughts into prayers with thanksgiving (believing He hears and will act), He will guard my heart and mind with peace (Phil. 4:6–7).

Christ said, "If you insist on saving your life, you will lose it. Only those who throw away their lives for my sake and for the sake of the Good News will ever know what it means to really live" (Mark 8:35 TLB). Let go! Choose to trust, and you will begin to really live.

The abundant life is what Christ purchased for us on Calvary. Satan, the "thief" who has come to "steal, kill and destroy" (John 10:10 TLB), specifically seeks to destroy this abundant life. Do not allow him to steal from you any longer. Choose now to face your fear, envy, discontentment, unforgiveness, or whatever it may be that the enemy and your flesh are using to cripple you. Come to the altar of sacrifice and choose to die to yourself that you might come alive through Christ.

Do you want to "leave ordinary," to be free of the chains of the mundane? Christ said, "You will know the truth, and the truth will make you free" (John 8:32 NASB). Believe the truth about what God has said, and turn to Him in prayer. Watch what Christ will do!

QUESTIONS TO CONSIDER

1. What sin is holding you back from the abundant life that Christ promised?

2. Confess the sin that the Holy Spirit has revealed. Choose to believe Christ and take any thoughts of doubt or unbelief captive (2 Cor. 10:3–5).

3. What steps will you take to obey Christ in this area of your life?

NOTES

CHAPTER SEVEN

THE LAVER

(EXODUS 30:17–21 NASB)

Let us draw near with true hearts
full of faith, with hearts rinsed clean
of any evil conscience, and with
bodies cleansed with pure water.

—Hebrews 10:22

After offering the sacrifices on the altar, the priest would move to the laver, or basin, which was filled with water. Here the priest would cleanse his hands and feet. As Louis Talbot said in *Christ in the Tabernacle,* "Now as the penalty of sin was judged at the brazen altar, so defilement was confessed and judged—put away—at the brazen laver."[1] The laver was made of the bronze mirrors of the women who worked at the doorway of the tent of meeting, or as The Voice translation calls it, the "congregation tent" (Ex. 38:8). It depicts the Word of God that washes and cleanses us (John 15:3).

Only the priests could wash their hands and feet at the laver. And you could only be a priest if you were born into the lineage of Aaron. When the priests washed at the laver and looked into it, they saw themselves.

James tells us that we are to look intently into the perfect law. We are not to be like the natural man, who looks at himself in the mirror and then leaves, forgetting what he saw (James 1:23–25). We are to allow the Word to reveal and to cleanse. We are to be doers of the Word and not just hearers (James 1:22).

I teach Bible studies through our women's ministry at church. One extremely busy Wednesday, I picked our youngest daughter up from school after cheerleading practice, and we rushed home to change clothes, grab a bite to eat, and head back out the door to get to church on time. I had gone into my bedroom to change clothes. I put on a skirt and then grabbed a couple of different pairs of shoes to decide which would work best. I put one of each shoe on my feet and stood in front of our full-length mirror . . . and then I left.

Later, Bethany and I were walking down the hallway at church, and I thought, *My feet sure do feel funny*. I looked down, and to my dismay, I had on two different shoes—two *very* different shoes!

Obviously, at this point there was nothing I could do about it. I walked right through our large west lobby and up the staircase and into my classroom. I knew that the sanguine personalities (the otter in Gary Smalley's book about temperaments—he loves people and is the life of the party[2]) in my class would never notice my shoes. But I also knew a melancholy (the beaver; think detail oriented—accountant[3]) would notice right away! Sure enough, one of my ladies walked up and asked as she pointed, "That was intentional—right?"

I laughed out loud and said, "I wish I could say it was!"

But of course there was a precious phlegmatic (the golden retriever—loyal and merciful[4]) who intentionally wore two different shoes the next week and sat on the front row. She didn't want me to be all alone in my shoe foible. Bless her sweet heart! (This is a Southern phrase that can be used indiscriminately to mean anything from "Isn't she sweet!" to "She just doesn't know any better.")

How had I missed seeing my mismatched footwear? I had looked in the mirror. But I left, forgetting what I looked like. When we look in God's Word, we are not to forget what we see. We are to leave changed.

> We must be born-again children of God if we are to gaze into the Word of God and see with "spirit" eyes.

Just as men had to be born into the priestly line before they were qualified to receive certain privileges and duties, we must be born-again children of God if we are to gaze into the Word of God and see with "spirit" eyes. It is only to those who have become part of the family of God that He grants access to the Holy Place.

This laver made of mirrors was the place where the priests washed their hands and feet before ministering to the Lord. It is here that we, too, will be cleansed. Jesus is the Word of God made flesh (John 1:1, 14). He is also the living water that becomes like rivers of living water within believers (John 7:38). He cleanses us as we gaze intently into His reflection.

Without washing, the priests dared not serve or worship, lest they die (Ex. 30:19–21). Without cleansing in the water of His Word, we will not be fit for worship or service. We are to worship Him in Spirit and truth (John 4:23). Jesus died to make us clean, and He lives to sanctify and cleanse us that He might present us to the Father without spot or blemish (Eph. 5:27).

Ephesians 5:26 states that Christ is sanctifying us, "having cleansed [us] by the washing of water with the word" (NASB). In John 17:17, Jesus prayed, asking the Father to sanctify us in His truth—"Your Word is truth" (NASB). As we immerse ourselves in His Word, we are renewed in our minds. Only by knowing the truth are we able to discern the lies of the evil one and the anti-God world system in which we live.

We arm ourselves with the Word of God. That is why it is so important to have a daily time when you meet with the Lord and systematically read through His Word. Making this discipline a priority in your life will change you from the inside out.

I recommend a one-year Bible reading plan, *The One Year Bible*, or *The One Year Chronological Bible*. These Bibles are divided in sections by day of the year. It takes about fifteen minutes to read one section. There are 96 fifteen-minute segments in each day. Can you give God 1/96th of your day?

> "God is your greatest fan. As your heavenly Father, He is constantly coaxing you forward into the heights of spiritual victory."
>
> —Bob Sorge

I suggest that you have a specific time and place that you meet with the Lord. Keep your Bible there as well as your prayer notebook, journal, and devotional. Open your Bible expecting to hear from God. Read slowly and intentionally. Consider the context, and try to put yourself in the place of the people you read about.

There will be times that a verse will appear to be in bold print. You will sense that God is speaking to you. Stop and reread the verse. I keep five-by-seven cards in the basket in my special place so I can write down verses that the Lord uses to speak to me. Write down your verse, take it with you, and meditate on it throughout the day. Allow the Word of God to renew your mind (Rom. 12:2). As you dwell on His Word, God will grant you understanding and often give you a new revelation of His character and will.

Christ is our great High Priest, who has opened up the way for us to minister to the Lord. We can be confident as we come before the Lord that His Spirit will reveal anything we need to confess and be cleansed from. As Hebrews says, "Since we have a great priest over the house of God, let us draw near with a sincere heart in full assurance of faith, having our hearts sprinkled clean from an evil conscience and our bodies washed with pure water" (10:21–22 NASB).

We are washed completely in the blood of Christ at salvation. But, just like the priests of the tabernacle, we have "daily dirt" that accumulates and needs to be washed in the water of His Word. As we confess our sins, "He is faithful and righteous to forgive us our sins and to cleanse us from all unrighteousness" (1 John 1:9 NASB). Cleansed

> "When you neglect the secret place, He's not disappointed in you, He's disappointed for you."
>
> —Bob Sorge

from our sins through confession, we no longer "grieve" or "quench" (Eph. 4:30; 1 Thess. 5:19) the Holy Spirit. It is through honest and humble confession that we are able to obey God's command, "You are to be holy, for I am holy" (1 Peter 1:16; Lev. 11:44; 19:2; 21:8; 22:32). This doesn't mean we will reach a point of sinless perfection. It does mean we are granted, through Christ, the ability to walk blamelessly with our God.

Your daily time with the Lord in His Word and presence is the most important appointment of your day! "God is your greatest fan. As your heavenly Father, He is constantly coaxing you forward into the heights of spiritual victory. When you neglect the secret place, He's not disappointed in you, He's disappointed for you."[5]

Allow the mirror of the Word to reveal all that the Holy Spirit is teaching you. Cleanse yourself in the washing of His Word as you confess your sins and "walk in a manner worthy of the Lord, to please Him in all respects" (Col. 1:10 NASB).

QUESTIONS TO CONSIDER

1. Do you have a specific time and place that you meet with the Lord?

2. What has the Lord "shown" you lately through His Word?

3. Share a verse that you are memorizing or meditating on that the Lord has used in your life.

NOTES

CHAPTER EIGHT

THE LAMPSTAND
(EXODUS 25:31-40)

"You are like that illuminating light. Let
your light shine everywhere you go, *that you
may illumine creation,* so men and women
everywhere may see your good actions, *may
see creation at its fullest, may see your
devotion to Me,* and may turn and praise
your Father in heaven *because of it.*"

–Matthew 5:16

The priest entered the enclosed section of the tabernacle
called the Holy Place every morning and evening. Inside this enclo-
sure he would encounter the lampstand, the table of showbread,
and the altar of incense. The lampstand was made of one piece of
pure hammered gold. It was fashioned into a stand with a central
shaft and six branches going out on the sides, three branches on
each side. The cups were shaped like almond blossoms, and only
pure oil of beaten olives was to be used. The lamp was to burn

continually and provided light for the ministering priests. Coals from the bronze altar were used to light the lamp.

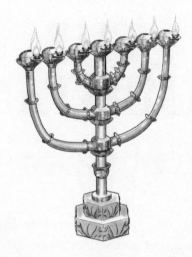

The Holy Place had four coverings: from the inside to the outside—embroidered linen, black goat skins, ram's skins dyed red, and badger skin. From the outside, the tabernacle looked like any other tent. The outer covering of badger skins was a type of leather that the people used to make their shoes. Could this be one reason the Lord allowed the Israelites' shoes not to wear out while they were in the desert (Deut. 8:4)? They had given this leather to the Lord for His tabernacle.

Only the priests saw the beauty of the interior. Similarly, only those who prepare their hearts and enter into the Spirit-filled life will ever see the true beauty of their relationship with Christ. Once inside, the priests could see by the light of the lamp, which illumined the beautifully embroidered linen covering. Imagine the light reflecting off of the gold of the lampstand, the table, and the altar.

The lampstand was the only source of light in the Holy Place—there was no natural light inside. Like the priests of old, we are not to walk in natural light. Our natural reasoning is not to govern our lives. Instead, we are to walk in the light of God's Word, guided by His Spirit. Only those who have been born of the Spirit and understand the things of the Spirit will experience this light. The Bible is very clear that the natural man "does not accept the things of the Spirit of God, for they are foolishness to him; and he cannot understand them, because they are spiritually appraised" (1 Cor. 2:14 NASB). This is revelation: for us to be allowed to see what our Lord sees.

> Should God be merciful to us and grant us even a small mea-sure of revelation, so that we can see ourselves as we are seen by Him, we shall immediately be smitten to the ground. We need not try to be humble. Those who live in the light cannot be proud. It is only while dwelling in darkness that we can be proud. Outside of God's light men can be arrogant and haughty; but under the revelation of the light they can only prostrate themselves before Him.[1]

Therein lies the difference between information and revelation. The Pharisees and Sadducees had a lot of information about the Scriptures. But it takes the revelation of the Spirit to understand and know the One to whom the Scriptures point. This is the very thing for which the Lord rebuked religious leaders. He said, "Here you are scouring through the Scriptures, hoping that you will find eternal life among a pile of scrolls. *What you don't seem to understand is that* the Scriptures point to Me" (John 5:39).

In Revelation 2:1, John described a dramatic vision in which he saw seven lampstands that represented seven churches. The letters the Lord penned through him to these churches were filled with instruction, encouragement, and rebuke. God threatened to remove the lamp in one of the churches if they did not repent (Rev. 2:5).

> "Not a single ray of light was allowed to come from the outside by the light of nature. The oil in the light, representing the Holy Spirit, was the only source of light by which the priest was to serve in the tabernacle."
>
> – M. R. DeHaan

These words remind us of Christ's words from the Sermon on the Mount. He said, "Let your light shine before men in such a way that they may see your good works, and glorify your Father who is in heaven" (Matt. 5:16 NASB).

The priests were responsible for cleaning, filling, and lighting the lamp each evening and morning. We, too, are responsible for making sure we are filled with the Spirit and that our lights are shining for a lost world to see. The lamp was to burn "continually" (Ex. 27:20) and never be extinguished. Likewise, we are to "shine like stars across the land" (Phil. 2:15) until we see Jesus.

We are commanded in Ephesians 5:18 to be filled with the Holy Spirit. Specifically, the verse tells us not to be "drunk with wine"— but to be "filled with the Spirit" (NASB). There is an obvious contrast being made. What happens to a person who is drunk? He walks differently (which is why a person suspected of being drunk will be asked to walk a straight line). He talks differently—his speech is slurred, or he says things he might otherwise filter and choose not to say. He responds differently—often having delayed responses or overreacting to a situation or person.

If we are to properly apply this contrast, it means that when we are filled with the Spirit, we will walk differently, talk differently, and respond differently. The Spirit controls us when we are filled by Him. The New Testament is clear that we are to live the *Spirit-filled* life as believers.

The priests were anointed with oil as they were set apart for service to the Lord. This oil represented the Holy Spirit, who would empower them for service. The Holy Spirit anointed Christ at His baptism. As believers we receive the Holy Spirit at conversion but must continually be filled with the Holy Spirit (Eph. 5:18).

As we walk in the Spirit, God will order our steps and illumine our paths. Psalm 119:105 says, "Your Word is a lamp to my feet and a light to my path" (NASB). Dr. M. R. DeHaan, in his book *The Tabernacle*, said, "Not a single ray of light was allowed to come from the outside by the light of nature. The oil in the light, representing the Holy Spirit, was the only source of light by which the priest was to serve in the tabernacle. The light of the candlestick points both to the Lord Jesus Christ, and also to the written Word of God, the two being inseparable."[2]

Dr. DeHaan also asserts that the central shaft represents Christ. The six branches represent us as His followers, who are "the light of the world" (Matt. 5:14): "Six is the number of man. The six branches are the men and women, the boys and the girls, united to Christ by faith, and made one in Him. Seven branches, but one candlestick. Seven is the number of perfection and all believers are by their union to Christ made perfect in Him, nourished by the oil of the Holy Spirit and kept forever."[3]

> "The light of the candlestick points both to the Lord Jesus Christ, and also to the written Word of God, the two being inseparable."
>
> — M. R. DeHaan

Individually, we are to be lights, and corporately as His body, we are to shine. May the whole world see the Light—may we never be guilty of hiding His light. Pray for boldness to live as "children of God above reproach in the midst of a crooked and perverse generation, among whom you appear as lights in the world" (Phil. 2:15 NASB).

QUESTIONS TO CONSIDER

1. Are you filled with the Holy Spirit and allowing God's Word to instruct you and light your path?

2. How is God using you to be a light in this dark world?

NOTES

CHAPTER NINE

THE TABLE OF SHOWBREAD

(EXODUS 25:23–30)

"I am the living bread that has come down
from heaven *to rescue those who eat it.*
Anyone who eats this bread will live forever.
The bread that I will give breathes life
into the cosmos. This bread is my flesh."

—John 6:51

The next article the priest would encounter upon entering the tabernacle was the table of showbread. It is also called the bread of the Presence and is literally translated the "bread of the face."[1] The table was made of acacia wood and covered with gold. Even the construction materials remind us of our Lord; the acacia wood "is a hard, incorruptible, indestructible wood that grows in the Sinai Desert. It beautifully portrays the humanity of Christ, who came from 'a root out of a dry ground' (Isa. 53:2) and was sinless in His human nature (Heb. 4:15; 7:26)."[2] The gold depicts His deity.

There was a rim around the edge and a ring on each corner of the table. The staves were made of wood and covered with gold for carrying the table when the Lord told the Israelites it was time to move.

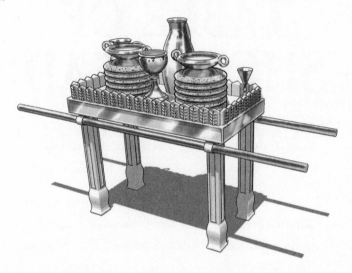

Twelve loaves of bread representing the twelve tribes of Israel were placed on the table each Sabbath. The bread that was removed was food for the priests who were ministering (Lev. 24:5–9). This bread represents Jesus, who said He was the Bread of Life, the Bread come down from heaven (John 6:35, 51). The priests placed frankincense on each row as a "memorial portion for the bread, even an offering by fire to the LORD" (Lev. 24:7 NASB). The frankincense is a beautiful reminder of our Lord, who manifested the sweet aroma of sinless perfection. We are to represent Him to the world and be the "fragrance of Christ to God among those who are being saved and among those who are perishing" (2 Cor. 2:15 NASB). It is interesting to note that the wise men brought frankincense as a gift to the Christ child (Matt. 2:11) in the town of Bethlehem, which means "house of bread."

The bread was to be made of fine flour ground and baked without leaven. Leaven in Scripture most often represents sin. The bread of the Presence depicts the body of our Lord, who was completely sinless—"who has been tempted in all things as we are, yet without sin" (Heb. 4:15 NASB). This bread also reminds us of the bread that was eaten without leaven on the night of the Passover. The people were to eat standing up with their shoes on, "dressed and ready to go *at a moment's notice*" (Ex. 12:11).

The priests who ministered in the tabernacle did not sit down. There was not a chair for them to recline in. They were to eat standing and to be ready to do the Lord's bidding. As they broke the bread, it pointed to the body of our Lord, who would be broken for us. It is Christ's broken body that is the Bread of Life! It is in brokenness that life is poured out. As we, too, are broken, God's Spirit is released to guide us to Him and His plan for our lives.

> It is in brokenness that life is poured out.

Life on this planet can drain the life right out of you! There are days when the pain of suffering, abuse, and misuse of humans seems to press down until it's hard to breathe. There have been times in my own life when I felt as though I were drowning and just couldn't quite make it to the top to gasp for air. It was as though someone or something were holding me under. Have you ever wanted to give up—to walk out on God? And yet, you couldn't. You couldn't, not because you are good or chose to make the right choice, but because He wouldn't let go of you (John 10:28–29). You have been sealed until the day of redemption (Eph. 1:13), and God is working in you to complete what He began when you became His (Phil. 1:6). What great confidence and encouragement these truths provide, especially in times of great trial or sorrow!

Jesus was a man of sorrows. The fine flour used in the bread of Presence depicts His suffering. The wheat had to be ground and the bread passed through the fire to be baked. Jesus understands the fire of suffering. We desire to "know Him and the power of His resurrection," but not necessarily "the fellowship of His sufferings" (Phil. 3:10 NASB). But it is the fire that purifies us and draws the dross of our own lives to the surface. The Father is conforming us to the image of His dear Son. As you have often heard, God is more concerned with our character than our comfort.

> It is the fire that purifies us and draws the dross of our own lives to the surface. The Father is conforming us to the image of His dear Son.

Devi Titus wrote a wonderful book entitled *The Table Experience*. In her research she came across an interesting fact pertaining to the table of the Presence. As she studied the table in the tabernacle, she found that this was the first table of this type to ever exist. Titus, who has a background in interior design, also discovered that "the height of the table in the tabernacle was the same height as our dining tables today."[3]

She went on to say, "As far as I can tell, I am not aware of any documentation in recorded history of a table of this size ever being built before God gave this exact description to Moses. And now the table is a central part of most cultures."[4] Tables even in the time of Christ were low, and the people reclined around them to eat.

It is at the table that the priests would fellowship with the Lord and with each other as they partook of the bread in a holy place

(Lev. 24:9). So like our tables today! Some of the fondest memories of my childhood are the conversations around our dinner table after a meal. To this day, when we have a meal at my parents' home, we linger around the table to enjoy each other's presence. My mother constantly amazes me by always having enough food for one more person. Everyone is welcome around her table.

Titus also included research in her book by journalist Miriam Weinstein, the author of *The Surprising Power of Family Meals.* Weinstein's book "draws on studies from psychology, education, nutrition, and sociology regarding the cultural phenomenon of family meals. Her thorough study of this subject led Weinstein to the surprising and bold conclusion that eating family meals together is a 'magic bullet' that dramatically improves 'the quality of your daily life, your children's chances of success in the world, your family's health, [and] our values in society."[5]

When Christian families gather around the table for a meal, they pause to thank the Lord for His provision and to invite His presence to join them. Weinstein also noted that along with all of the benefits mentioned, "eating family meals at the table also seems to have a unique spiritual significance. She observes, 'Each time we say grace, we are including another presence at our table—God comes to dinner.'"[6]

Deuteronomy 6:4–9 is known as the *Shema* (Hebrew for "hear"), and it contains the mandate from God for families. First they were to love the Lord with all their hearts, souls, and might. The proof of their love would be in their obedience to His commands and their diligence to pass them on to their children. Talk about God's commands was to happen "when you sit in your house and when you walk by the way and when you lie down and when you rise up" (Deut. 6:7 NASB). Conversations about God and what He requires should be as natural as talking about any other subject that is dear to us. Since we are to love God first and foremost, He should be our favorite topic of conversation.

I heard a speaker say recently that 80 percent of churchgoing families do not have values-based conversations during the week. Could it be that the busyness of our culture has subtly stolen time at the dinner table and we have unknowingly given up one of the primary ways and places we pass on our values and beliefs? There is only one way to regain that influence. We must prioritize our lives and clear our calendars of the things that rob our families, and reinstitute family mealtime.

I have a sweet friend whose husband teasingly says, "When my wife says it's time for dinner, the children all go get in the van." Unfortunately for so many families, too many meals are on the go, forfeiting communion as a family as well as nutrition.

When our children were at home and involved in extracurricular activities, it became more of a challenge to guard that time. But each month my husband and I would sit down with our calendars and block out date nights, family nights, and family meals. Some nights the meal needed to be early; other nights it may be late. But we were diligent to protect that time. I didn't fully understand the significance at the time, but I knew it was a very special part of my childhood and one that I wanted my children to experience as well.

It is such a blessing today to see our three married children carrying on that same tradition. And what a joy it is when they all gather around our table and four generations are able to enjoy each other's company and bask in the presence of the One who has made it all possible.

Christ is able to multiply the loaves of bread and feed the hungry multitudes. His table is open to all who will come through the door and to the brazen altar of the cross. Jesus said, "I am the living bread that has come down from heaven *to rescue those who eat it.* Anyone who eats this bread will live forever. The bread that I will give breathes life into the cosmos. This bread is My flesh" (John 6:51).

In the Old Testament, Jesus was the manna that fed the Israelites daily. He was enough for every day. Jesus told His followers in the Sermon on the Mount that we are not to worry about tomorrow, for each day has enough trouble of its own (Matt. 6:34). We are to focus on today and live it for His glory. He will take care of our tomorrows; in fact, He is already there.

Deuteronomy 8:3 tells us, "He humbled you by making you hungry *when there was no food in the desert.* Then He fed you with manna, a food you and your ancestors had never heard of. He did this because He wanted you to understand that what makes you truly alive is not the bread you eat but following every word that comes from the mouth of the Eternal One."

> "The Word descends from our minds into our hearts and there finds a dwelling place."
>
> —Henri Nouwen

Jesus quoted this very verse when the enemy tempted Him to turn the stones to bread in the wilderness. Jesus is the Word who became flesh. He is the Word that feeds our hungry souls and strengthens our inner man. Henri Nouwen said, "By the Word of God we are formed into living Christs, and this formation goes far beyond information, instruction, edification, or inspiration. This formation requires eating the Word, chewing on it, digesting it, and thus letting it become true nourishment. Thus the Word descends from our minds into our hearts and there finds a dwelling place."[7]

Revelation 2:17 tells us that those who overcome will receive the hidden manna. And until that day, we are to remember and commemorate what Christ did for us at Calvary. As Christ instituted the Lord's Supper, breaking the bread and passing it out to the disciples, He said, "This is My body, My body given for you. Do this to remember Me" (Luke 22:19).

The breaking of the bread (symbolizing His body) and the drinking of the juice (symbolizing His blood) remind us of the great sacrifice Christ made on our behalf. We reflect on His sacrifice and examine our lives so that we don't take the Lord's Supper with unconfessed sin in our lives (1 Cor. 11:27–32). To knowingly partake with unconfessed sin would be to take it in an unworthy manner. The Bible is clear that the Lord disciplines those who do.

The table represented the fellowship of His presence and pointed to Christ as the Bread of Life. As we partake of Him, we become one with Him. In Him, our hungering souls are satisfied, freeing us to love others and invite them to the banquet table the Lord has set for all who will come.

QUESTIONS TO CONSIDER

1. How often do you reflect upon Christ as the Bread of Life, and how do you allow Him to nourish and strengthen you in your inner man?

2. How are you intentionally living out Deuteronomy 6:4–9?

3. What can you do to protect and provide mealtime for your family? How can you make it a time for passing on your values and beliefs?

NOTES

CHAPTER TEN

THE ALTAR OF INCENSE

(EXODUS 30:1–16, 34–38)

And when He took it, the four living
creatures and twenty-four elders
fell prostrate before the Lamb. *They
worshiped Him, and* each one held a harp
and golden bowls filled with incense
(the prayers of God's holy people).

–Revelation 5:8

The altar of incense was placed before the veil that separated
the Holy Place from the Holy of Holies. It was made of acacia wood
and covered with gold. It was the same shape as the brazen altar,
but smaller. It had a horn at each corner. Burning coals from the
brazen altar were brought to light the incense that was offered each
morning and evening.

This altar was the last article before the veil that separated the priests from the ark of the covenant. The veil of fine twisted linen with beautifully embroidered cherubim of blue, purple, and scarlet depicted the colors and the glory of the throne room of God. It was here that Aaron, the high priest, would offer incense as he prayed for the people.

Incense in Scripture often represents prayer. The altar of incense points to Christ, our great High Priest, who ever lives to make intercession for us (Rom. 8:34). Revelation 4–5 gives us a very vivid description of the throne room. Revelation 5:8 tells us our prayers are held in golden bowls before the throne, and they continually rise before the Lord like incense. The psalmist said, "Consider my prayer as *an offering of* incense *that rises* before You" (Ps. 141:2).

Your prayers are eternal because they are tangible in heaven. The Bible says they continually rise before the Lord. Not just once, when they are prayed, but continually. God begins to move when we ask, seek, and knock. When we are faithful to pray, He is faithful to answer. Your prayers are the one thing that can outlive you. Prayers you are praying today can still be reverberating through the years, should Jesus tarry.

When we pray, God begins to orchestrate things in the spirit realm that eventually manifest in the physical. I have an uncle for whom we prayed over a period of several years. He was diagnosed with cancer. As I prayed for him, there was an overwhelming sense that I was to present the gospel to him.

I asked my small group Bible study to pray for me during an upcoming family reunion. We were going to be spending a week in cabins at a lake in Arkansas. I knew there would be about eighty of us there, and finding my uncle by himself would be a challenge.

I was walking out of our cabin one morning with my sister and saw my uncle Henry sitting on the patio by himself. I was carrying my third child, not yet a year old. I nearly tossed my daughter to my sister and said, "Pray!"

I sat down beside my uncle and began to ask him about his physical condition. He had cancer of the throat, and his voice box had been removed. He spoke with an electrolarynx. I told him I was concerned about him physically, but my greatest concern was about his spiritual condition. As I began to share the gospel, big tears rolled down his cheeks. He did

> When we pray, God begins to orchestrate things in the spirit realm that eventually manifest in the physical.

not commit his life to Christ that morning, but he promised me he would.

We drove into the little town later that afternoon, and I found a Christian bookstore. I bought him a Bible in a modern translation and purchased a card that contained the plan of salvation. I wrote in the card how much I loved him and wanted to know that we would all be having a real family reunion one day in heaven.

My Bible study group was faithful to pray for Henry. Many of them sent him cards telling him they were praying for him. A few weeks later my uncle was back in the hospital. I called my aunt to check on him. I was going to Bible study and wanted to be able to give a report. When my aunt answered the phone, she began to yell, "Henry got saved! Henry got saved!"

> Do not believe the accuser of the brethren, who tries to convince you that your prayers are going no higher than the ceiling.

My aunt's pastor had come by to visit Henry in the hospital and asked him about his salvation. Henry told the pastor he had committed his life to Christ and was a changed man. This happened just months before God called my uncle home. The faithful prayers of his wife and the prayers of all those who had called out his name to the Lord were answered by our gracious God.

Do not believe the accuser of the brethren, who tries to convince you that your prayers are going no higher than the ceiling. He will try to tell you that you are far too weak spiritually or soiled with sin to ever make a difference when you pray. Praise the Lord, we don't come before God in our own righteousness, but in the very righteousness of Jesus Christ (2 Cor. 5:21).

We can learn so much about prayer if we study the life of Christ. He would often slip away into the wilderness to pray. His prayer life was so vibrant and so different from anything the disciples had experienced that they asked Him to teach them to pray (Luke 11:1). It was after this request that the Lord gave them the model prayer, or what many call the Lord's Prayer.

This prayer was really not meant to be memorized and repeated, but instead to be used as a model or example of how to pray. Prayer is about relationship. It is a conversation with the Father through the Son, empowered by the Spirit. Prayer is not an activity on our "to do" lists. It is intended to be a two-way conversation. We are to listen to God through His Word. We are also to lift our requests to Him and then listen as He responds through His Word and His Spirit.

It is when we are faithful to pray that we begin to experience intimacy with Christ. The better we know Him, the more we will love Him. The more we love Him, the more we desire to obey and glorify Him. The greater the love, the greater the level of holiness (John 14:21). Obedience always precedes blessing and further revelation.

God's desire has always been to be known by His creation. Before the tabernacle, God had spoken and revealed Himself to a few individuals. But through the tabernacle, God was now in the midst of His people, and they were able to see His presence and follow His lead.

Through prayer, God allows us to know Him and to hear His voice. What He says is so much more important than anything I could ever say to Him. One Word from Him can lift a heavy load, heal a wounded spirit, or empower for a new kingdom exploit. God has not called us to the ordinary but to the *extraordinary* that can only be explained by His presence.

Prayer is our power line. Without it we will never have the power of the Spirit to fulfill God's plan for our lives. My husband loves the book of Acts. He has often said that the only difference between the church of Acts and the church of the twenty-first century is prayer. We preach the same message and we sing similar songs. But first-century Christians were dedicated to prayer (Acts 2:42). They were known for their prayer lives. In my husband's book, *Pray Like It Matters*, he stated that "the early church was literally birthed in a prayer meeting."[1]

It was when the disciples were "ministering to the Lord and fasting" (Acts 13:2 NASB) that the Holy Spirit said, "'Commission Barnabas and Saul to a project I have called them to accomplish.' They fasted and prayed some more, laid their hands on the two selected men, and sent them off on their new mission" (vv. 13:2–3). Thus, not only the church but missions itself was birthed in a prayer meeting!

Another time, after being threatened, the disciples were gathered together praying. The room where they were praying was shaken, and they were all filled with the Holy Spirit and began to speak the Word of God with boldness (Acts 4:31). We cannot expect God to entrust the true riches of His Spirit to prayerless people.

In *Secrets of the Secret Place,* Bob Sorge says:

> Hell will do everything in its power to misrepresent and distort the exuberant delight of this dynamic reality; this present world system is strategically designed to squeeze out your time and energy for the secret place; the church usually focuses its best energies on getting saints busy; and there seem to be relatively few believers whose secret life with God is so vibrantly

life-giving that it kindles a contagious desire in others to follow their example.[2]

Through the years, I have been drawn to others with this vibrant relationship. I have been blessed by the Lord to have had people in my life who were great prayer warriors: men and women who walked intimately with the Lord. I like to describe them as people that "God talks to." You know who they are. They are the very ones you want praying for you when you have a crisis.

At our first church, I was drawn to a couple who lived and walked by faith. I cherish the time we spent together sharing about Christ and praying with one another. His parents had been missionaries and were humble people of great faith. One Christmas we were invited to their home to spend time with their extended family. Our one-month-old daughter had a cold and was very congested. His mother placed her on her shoulder, with her hand on her head, and began to pray for her. Immediately, the congestion was gone!

In our second church, it was Mrs. Elizabeth. She is the mother of one of my dear friends from college. Mrs. Elizabeth walks and talks with God. He speaks to her and reveals great truths to her. Several times I asked her to meet me for lunch or brunch, and I would take a Bible and a notepad. I would ask her questions and record her answers. When we were preparing to move to Alabama, I called Mrs. Elizabeth and asked if we could meet and pray. I wanted her to pray for me. It was at this time that I knew the Lord was wanting me to face the fear of speaking in

> "This present world system is strategically designed to squeeze out your time and energy for the secret place."
>
> —Bob Sorge

front of adults and to step out in faith and obedience. I didn't tell Mrs. Elizabeth what I was struggling with, but the Lord told her. That was the beginning of my freedom from fear.

In our third church, the Lord allowed me to meet and be able to learn from Sylvia Gunter, author of *Prayer Portions* and *Living in His Presence.* Sylvia is a giant of the faith, who knows God and walks with God in power and revelation.

Sylvia was so gracious to allow me to meet with her and to observe as she prayed with and ministered to women. She also taught and trained our women's ministry leadership how to pray with women and help them find healing and freedom. This group of women became some of my dearest friends as we prayed and learned together.

At our current church, God brought together a group of women who have met monthly to pray for my family and me. We soon became a sweet and intimate prayer circle, lifting up each other's families and our church on a regular basis. I depend on their faithful prayers and am so grateful for their authentic relationship with Christ.

I will never feel that I have "arrived" in prayer. This relationship will continue to grow and challenge me until I see Jesus. But I am so dependent upon my time with the Lord that I cannot go through my day without that time with my Savior. I choose to sit at His feet and then to commune with Him throughout the day. This is what I believe Paul was talking about when he told the Thessalonians to "pray without ceasing" (1 Thess. 5:17 NASB).

The altar of incense is the place where the priests ministered to the Lord every morning and evening. The incense rose to the Lord just as our prayers rise before Him. How full is the golden bowl of your prayers before His throne?

Oswald Chambers said, "The essential meaning of prayer is that it nourishes the life of the Son of God in me and enables Him to manifest Himself in my mortal flesh."[3] Our greatest desires should be to know God and to be conformed to the image of Christ. Prayer accomplishes both.

QUESTIONS TO CONSIDER

1. Who has impacted your prayer life?

2. Begin to meet and pray with another believer or believers. Or ask a woman whose walk with Christ you respect to meet and pray with you.

NOTES

CHAPTER ELEVEN

THE VEIL

(EXODUS 26:31-35)

He has created for us a new and
living way through the curtain,
that is, through His flesh.

—Hebrews 10:20

The veil was the curtain that separated the Holy Place from
the Holy of Holies. It represents the separation between man and
God.

The veil was made of fine twined linen embroidered with blue,
purple, and scarlet threads. Cherubim were woven into the veil.

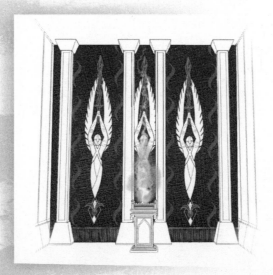

Many Bible scholars believe this veil or "curtain was actually a fine woven rug 4 inches thick, 60 feet high and 40 feet wide."[1]

The colors woven into the veil can be seen as a representation of Christ. The white linen reminds us of His sinless perfection. The blue is thought by some to represent His deity, since heaven is so often depicted by sapphire (Ex. 24:10). The purple shows His royalty, and the scarlet represents His blood.

Hebrews 10:20 tells us that the veil was the flesh of Jesus Christ. It is in Christ that divinity and humanity come together. While on the earth, Christ's flesh veiled His deity. On the Mount of Transfiguration, when Peter, James, and John were given a glimpse of His unveiled glory, "His face shone like the sun, and His garments became as white as light" (Matt. 17:2 NASB).

There were three curtains in the tabernacle. They basically served two functions. "The word *veil* (Heb., *Paroketh)* means to *separate* and describes its ministry. The veil acted as a barrier between God and man, shutting God in and man out (Lev. 16:2): and the curtains permitted access to worship after the priests had met the required conditions set forth in the Mosaic law."[2]

The three curtains were the gate of the courtyard, the gate of the tabernacle, and the veil that separated the Holy Place from the Holy of Holies. The veil with the interwoven cherubim was hung facing east, just as the cherubim with the flaming sword were placed on the east side of the garden of Eden, blocking the way back in and guarding the Tree of Life (Gen. 3:24).

Jennifer Kennedy Dean describes this beautifully in her book *Power in the Name of Jesus:*

> The veil hid the presence of Jehovah who alone is life. No one could enter behind the veil except by the prescribed way—with blood. The veil had cherubim worked into its design. The

cherubim cut off the way to the life, as in Eden . . . When Jesus died on the Cross, the veil was torn in two and the barrier became an opening. He is the way into abundant life. He walked through the flaming swords and let the sword pierce Him so that He could be our true and living way.[3]

Truly Christ is the way, the truth, and the life, and no one comes to the Father except through Him (John 14:6). His body was broken, opening the way for all to come through truth to the life given by the Father. When Christ's body was torn on Calvary and He gave up His spirit, God tore the veil in the temple from top to bottom. He opened the way into His presence through the shed blood of His Son.

The three curtains or entrances represent salvation and the maturation that occurs as we minister to the Lord according to His Word. We first enter through salvation at the gate of the courtyard and the altar (the cross). Unfortunately, so many stop in the courtyard and never get beyond their initial salvation.

Only the priests were allowed to enter the Holy Place. They were the only ones authorized. It is as we mature spiritually that we are authorized or eligible to enter into the abundant life that Christ died to purchase for us. It is here that we are filled with the Spirit, commune with God, and spend time with Him through prayer.

Those who enter through the third entrance enter into the very presence of God. It is with the upright that God is intimate. He shares the secret things with those who fear or revere Him

> It is with the upright that God is intimate. He shares the secret things with those who fear or revere Him.

(Ps. 25:14). "For the LORD is righteous, He loves righteousness; the upright will behold His face" (Ps. 11:7 NASB).

In a very uncertain time in my life, the Lord spoke to me through His manifest presence. In August 2000 my husband was diagnosed with myasthenia gravis. After his diagnosis, tests revealed he had a tumor on his thymus gland. This gland is below the sternum and must be removed by a procedure similar to open-heart surgery.

"I am your
Husband
and Father.
I am able."

—God

The night before his surgery, not knowing if the tumor was malignant or what the outcome would be, I was crying out to the Lord in prayer. I reminded the Lord that I needed my husband. I said, "Lord, our four children need their father."

Almost instantly, I sensed Him say, *"I am your Husband and Father. I am able."*

I literally held my hands out as though presenting my husband to the Lord and said, "Yes, Lord— You are able!" I knew then, regardless of what happened the next day, God would not leave me or forsake me. He is able and He is faithful!

My husband survived the surgery and the tumor was benign. He still battles myasthenia gravis, which causes extreme muscle weakness and fatigue, and he is dependent upon medicine to function. But he has continued to preach and pastor.

We continue to pray for his healing, but in the meantime, God has said, "My grace is enough to cover and sustain you. My power is made perfect in weakness" (2 Cor. 12:9). When I looked up the Greek word that is translated "weakness," I saw that it is the very word that was used to name the disease we are fighting: *asthenia*.

There have been times that Steve would be too weak to preach and yet God would take over when he stood behind the pulpit. He would preach with great power and strength. God is faithful, and He will provide us with whatever we need to fulfill His plan and call. If He has called you, He will provide you with all you need—even physical strength—when you meet Him behind the veil.

QUESTIONS TO CONSIDER

1. Do you ever feel that there is a thick veil between you and God? Do you think that you are still in the courtyard, lingering by the altar, or have you moved into the inner court?

2. Have you ever experienced the manifest presence of God? How would you describe it? He lives within you that you might know Him in all of His glory.

NOTES

CHAPTER TWELVE

THE ARK
OF THE
COVENANT
AND THE
MERCY SEAT

(EXODUS 25:10–22)

The Anointed One did not enter into
handcrafted sacred spaces—imperfect
copies of heavenly originals—but into
heaven itself, where He stands in the
presence of God on our behalf.

—Hebrews 9:24

Behind the veil in the tabernacle was the ark of the covenant or covenant chest. It was a box made of acacia wood and overlaid with gold. This construction can be interpreted to signify the humanity and the deity of Christ. As we discussed earlier, the durable wood reminds us of Christ's humanity, while the gold represents His deity. The ark contained the Ten Commandments, Aaron's rod, and a jar of manna. The mercy seat was the lid or covering of the box and was made of solid gold with a cherub on each end.

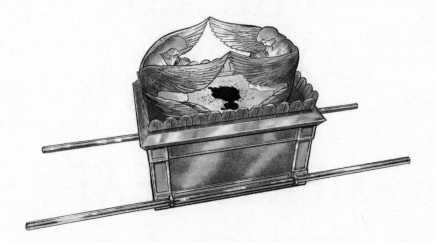

It was on the mercy seat that the high priest applied the blood on the Day of Atonement, and it was here that the Shekinah glory of God rested (Ex. 40:34–35; Rom. 3:25; Heb. 4:15–16; 9:6–7, 11–14). The ark and the mercy seat represent the very throne of God—the real mercy seat where the blood of Jesus was applied (Heb. 9:24–28).

The Lord told Moses in Exodus 25:22, "I will meet with you there. I will speak to you from above the seat of mercy between the two winged creatures that sit atop the covenant chest. *From there, I will speak to you* about all the commands *and instructions* I have for the people of Israel." God said of Moses, "With him I communicate face-to-face. We speak directly and without riddles. He can even see the very form of the Eternal" (Num. 12:8).

God also told Moses to tell Aaron "he cannot go whenever he wants beyond the veil to the holy place before the seat of mercy that covers the covenant chest" (Lev. 16:2). Aaron served as high priest, and he was only allowed behind the curtain one time a year, on the Day of Atonement.

On this day, Aaron would take off his beautiful high priest garments. He was to wear only the white linen tunic—the white signifying purity and forgiveness. He was to bring a young bull for a sin offering, a ram for a burnt offering, and two male goats. The goat chosen by lot as the sin offering would be sacrificed before the Lord. The goat chosen as the scapegoat would be presented alive before the Lord.

The young bull was a sin offering for Aaron and his family. The bull was offered and the blood was applied to the mercy seat and sprinkled before the ark. Then Aaron would take the blood of the sin offering (goat) for the people and sprinkle it on the mercy seat and before the ark. In this way he made atonement for the Israelites. No one was to come into the tent until Aaron came out.

Christ bore our sin in His body on Calvary, thus removing our sin from us. . . . Oh, what a Savior, High Priest, and King!

After the blood had been applied in the Holy Place, the tent of meeting, and on the brazen altar, Aaron would bring forth the live goat. He would lay his hands on the goat's head and confess the Israelites' sins and rebellion over the goat. A man chosen for the task would then take the goat out into the wilderness. The goat would carry away the sins of the people.

Next, Aaron was to go into the Tent of Meeting and take off the linen tunic, wash himself, and put on the garments of the high priest. He would then offer the burnt offering for himself and the burnt offering for the people, to make atonement for their sin. Finally, he would burn the fat of the sin offering.

On this day no man or woman was to do any work. The Israelites were to observe it as a Sabbath of rest. This was a lasting ordinance for Aaron and all the people. After this, the people's sins were covered before the Lord.

In Christ we see both the goat for sacrifice and the scapegoat. Jesus offered His sinless body in our place on the cross. The wages of sin is death (Rom. 3:23), and God paid our debt. But the Bible also tells us that Christ bore our sin in His body on Calvary, thus removing our sin from us "as far as east is from the west" (Ps. 103:12). Oh, what a Savior, High Priest, and King!

> The ark of the covenant was also called the ark of the testimony. As we enter the secret place, God will meet with us and grant us testimonies of His power and faithfulness.

The ark of the covenant was also called the ark of the testimony. As we enter the secret place, God will meet with us and grant us testimonies of His power and faithfulness. I have a testimony about God's miraculous provision that occurred while I was working on this manuscript.

A woman whom I had met only briefly (Linda) contacted me to speak at a retreat on prayer and intimacy with Christ. I shared with her about the work I was doing on the tabernacle and prayer. She became excited and asked if I was familiar with Betty Vick, who lived in Memphis and had taught on the tabernacle for more than thirty years. I was not, so she contacted Betty to see if she would be available for a meeting.

Not only were we able to meet, but Betty had the tabernacle that she had created for her teachings. It was made to scale and exactly like the biblical record. I was so awed by her work! She offered to let me use it sometime. She also offered to let me make a copy of her notes.

Linda spent the night with her niece in Memphis that night and was recounting the afternoon to her when her niece said, "Aunt Linda, you had me type those notes for Miss Betty fifteen or sixteen years ago. I think I might still have them."

Sure enough, she found the floppy disk where she had saved the notes. Linda immediately went to a print center, made a copy, and had them saved on a flash drive. She sent them to me the next morning. I have quoted Betty twice in this book and have been amazed by her insight.

God is always at work. But if we never make it to the secret place, we will not have much of a testimony. Our testimonies should not just be about when we were saved, but about what God is doing in our lives today.

QUESTIONS TO CONSIDER

1. What prayer has God answered for you recently?

2. What new truth is He revealing to you as you read His Word?

3. What are you trusting Christ for that only He can do?

NOTES

CHAPTER THIRTEEN

THE TEMPLE OF SOLOMON

A PERMANENT DWELLING

> "O Eternal One, Israel's God, there is
> no other God who compares to You in
> heaven or on earth. You have guarded Your
> covenant and revealed Your loyal love to
> those who serve You with all their being."
>
> —1 Kings 8:23

The tabernacle was temporary. It was a tent that the Israelites traveled with all over the wilderness, and eventually brought to the promised land in Shiloh. That tent/tabernacle lasted for almost five hundred years before Solomon's temple was built. The temporary tabernacle was a picture of our temporary bodies, which now house the Holy Spirit. These bodies will one day be glorified and in our forever home. During the reign of Solomon, the articles of the tabernacle would be replaced by the temple, giving the people a more permanent place to worship God.

After the period of the judges, the people cried out for a king. God gave them what they wanted. God had Samuel (the last of the judges and the first of the prophets) anoint Saul as the first king of Israel. Saul was exactly who the people thought they needed for a king. He was tall and handsome and, by all outward appearances, fit for the job. But his heart was revealed as he was tested by his position and found lacking.

God chose the second king. King David was a man after God's own heart, and he longed to build a temple, a permanent dwelling place for the Lord. Yet the Lord said to him, "No, you're not the one. You're a warrior. You've been a man who's shed blood. But I will allow your son, the one who follows you, to build a temple, a place for Me to dwell here in Jerusalem," the place that God chose (1 Chron. 22, paraphrased).

Although David was not allowed to build the temple, he began to gather the materials that his son Solomon would need and dedicated them to the Lord. In 1 Kings 8, the temple was built and prepared for dedication. Gifted artisans made the articles for the temple. First Kings 8:6 states, "Then the priests brought the ark of the covenant of the LORD to its place, into the inner sanctuary of the house" (NASB).

> The Israelites wandering in the wilderness were not allowed to enter the promised land ... because of unbelief. There are tremendous spiritual parallels between their journey in the desert and our individual journeys with God.

Reflect back on the tabernacle and envision the outer court, where the brazen altar was, where they offered the burnt offerings.

Next was the laver, where the priests would cleanse themselves with the water. Then they would go inside the Holy Place. In the Holy Place was the lampstand, the table of showbread, and the altar of incense. In the Most Holy Place, the Holy of Holies, they placed the ark.

If you look at descriptions of the throne room in Scripture, you will see that there are seraphim and cherubim flying around the throne of God, crying out, "Holy, holy, holy is the Lord God the Almighty" (Rev. 4:8 NIV). The cherubim on the mercy seat depict what is actually present and taking place around God's throne. We know from our study that the ark and the mercy seat represent the throne of God.

> For the cherubim spread their wings over the place of the ark, and the cherubim made a covering over the ark and its poles from above . . . There was nothing in the ark except the two tablets of stone which Moses put there at Horeb, where the LORD made a covenant with the sons of Israel, when they came out of the land of Egypt. It happened that when the priests came from the holy place, the cloud filled the house of the LORD, so that the priests could not stand to minister because of the cloud, for the glory of the LORD filled the house. (1 Kings 8:7–11 NASB)

What did the glory of the Lord go in with? Not with man's words, not with man's procession, not with man's prayers. The presence went into the Holy Place when the temple was set up exactly the way God told them to, and it came in over the ark. What did the ark contain? The Word of God—God's commands. His presence did not come in with man's words but with the Word of God. His presence so filled the temple that the priests had to back out. They couldn't even minister; they were so overwhelmed by the manifest presence of God.

Second Chronicles also records this same scene, and it tells us that fire came down at the same time and consumed the offerings (2 Chron. 7:1). We see the God of the cloud and the God of the fire once again. His holiness filled the temple, and He lit the fire of the brazen altar just as He had done for the tabernacle.

Then Solomon said, "The LORD has said that He would dwell in the thick cloud. I have surely built You a lofty house, a place for Your dwelling forever" (1 Kings 8:12–13 NASB). We see that Solomon then prayed. He asked the Lord to deliver his people should they ever let their hearts turn from Him. Finally, he blessed the whole assembly, and in 1 Kings 8:56, he said, "Blessed be the LORD, who has given rest to His people Israel" (NASB).

Hebrews tells us that the Israelites wandering in the wilderness were not allowed to enter the promised land, which is actually called God's "rest," because of unbelief (Heb. 4:1–2). There are tremendous spiritual parallels between their journey in the desert and our individual journeys with God. Just like the Israelites, when we do not believe we are not allowed to enter God's rest, that place of no anxiety, that place of abundance.

Solomon prayed a prayer that I have recorded in my prayer journal. I pray it many times after interceding for my family or our church. I repeat the words of Solomon as I request of the Lord, "Lord, may these words of mine, which I have made in supplication before You, be near to You, Lord, day and night, that You may maintain the cause of Your servant, and the cause of Your people [whether that cause concerns my family or the cause of Your people, Bellevue Baptist Church], as each day requires, so that all the peoples of the earth may know that the Lord is God, and there is no one else. Let their hearts therefore be wholly devoted to the Lord our God, to walk in His statutes and to keep His commandments, as at this day" (1 Kings 8:60–61, adapted from the NASB). Not for our glory—but for His alone!

What do we know about Solomon's reign? He started out great, didn't he? But unfortunately, he and his people would move very quickly from the dedication of the temple, and the manifest presence of God, to the desecration of the temple and the Word of God. And eventually God would remove His presence from His people and the kingdom would be divided.

God allowed the Assyrians to come in and conquer the Northern Kingdom. Then He allowed the Babylonians to come in and conquer the Southern Kingdom, all the while sending prophet after prophet after prophet to warn His people.

Isaiah was one of those prophets, as was Micah, Amos, Joel, Hosea and Jeremiah. What did the inhabitants of Israel and Judah do to the prophets? They ridiculed them, and they said, "No way. God would never allow a foreign nation to conquer Jerusalem." Do you know why they didn't believe the prophets? They had the temple. They were saying, in effect, "We've got God. He can't do anything to us; we have His temple!"

> So often, we don't know the God of the Bible because we don't study God's Word in its entirety.

Have you ever heard somebody say similar things about America? When preachers faithfully warn of God's coming judgment on our nation's sin, Americans cry, "How can that happen? We're America. We were founded on Christian principles." Aren't we living like the Israelites today? Do people in our own nation not ridicule men of God, prophets who stand up to speak the truth of God's Word? They say, "That's not going to happen. That's 'hate speech.' How could you even say things like that?"

And yet, God says, "This is My Word. You will do it My way or I will remove My presence, and I will then send My judgment." We can't change who God is or what He has said. It's who He has always been. So often, we don't know the God of the Bible because we don't study God's Word in its entirety.

When we do, we see He is the same yesterday, today, and forever (Heb. 13:8). He has not changed. Just as Solomon prayed for the people, may we love the Lord with all of our hearts. May we live according to His Word, and then we can intercede on behalf of our nation, and ask God to "forgive our sins, Lord. Forgive us so that you can then heal our land" (See 2 Chron. 7:14).

QUESTIONS TO CONSIDER

1. Are you interceding for your city and nation?

2. Ask the Lord to give you specific scriptures to pray for the lost, your city, and the nations.

NOTES

CHAPTER FOURTEEN

GOD'S GLORY COMES TO EARTH

Suddenly a messenger of the Lord
stood in front of them, and the
darkness was replaced by a glorious
light—the shining light of God's glory.

—Luke 2:9

After the Bible's record of the shekinah glory of God filling the temple that Solomon built, you will search the rest of the Old Testament in vain, seeking another recorded manifestation of the glory of God in the midst of His people. In fact, the world would not experience His glory again for some nine hundred years. Finally, at the opening of the New Testament, we read:

> In the same region there were some shepherds staying out in the fields and keeping watch over their flock by night. And an angel of the Lord suddenly stood before them, and the *glory of the Lord* shone around them; and they were terribly frightened. But the angel said to them, "Do not be afraid; for behold, I bring you good news of great joy which will be for all the people; for today

in the city of David there has been born for you a Savior, who is Christ the Lord. This will be a sign for you: you will find a baby wrapped in cloths and lying in a manger." And suddenly there appeared with the angel a multitude of the heavenly host praising God and saying, "Glory to God in the highest, and on earth peace among men with whom He is pleased." (Luke 2:8–14 NASB; emphasis added)

When the angels had departed, the shepherds hurried to the manger and found exactly what the angels had announced. They told Mary and Joseph about what they had seen and heard. The scripture tells us that Mary pondered all these things in her heart. The shepherds left glorifying God for what He had done.

From the announcement by the angel Gabriel that she would conceive to the announcement of Jesus' birth, Mary had many things to ponder and wonder about. These angelic announcements would be just the beginning of many miraculous manifestations.

John 1:1 says, "In the beginning was the Word, and the Word was with God, and the Word was God" (NASB). And verse 14 says, "And the Word became flesh, and dwelt among us, and we saw His glory, glory as of the only begotten from the Father, full of grace and truth" (NASB). The word translated "dwelt" in this passage is from the same root as the Greek word for "tent" or "tabernacle." It could quite literally be translated "tabernacled among us."

Everything in the Old Testament, including the tabernacle and temple, pointed to Jesus Christ. He is the fulfillment. He was able to say to the Pharisees and the Sadducees who desired to destroy Him, "Someone greater than the temple is here. I am greater than the temple. I am the fulfillment of the temple." (See Matthew 12:1–8.) How sad that those who so loved the temple were the very ones who would crucify the One to whom that temple pointed.

How dangerous it is to love a building or a tradition or religion more than we love the One who came to save us! May we be careful that we are not deceived, as the Pharisees were, because the temple has now come in a Person.

God put Himself in our place through His Son and bore our sin. As Christ took our place at Calvary, He opened the door for us to experience intimacy and oneness with the Father. He purchased for us a right relationship—a restoration of the lost intimacy.

After Jesus' death and resurrection, how did He leave the earth? Into what did He ascend, according to Acts 1? He ascended into a cloud. And what did the angels say to the followers? "Don't stand here gawking at the sky. You've got things to do."

Jesus left like this. Guess what? He's coming back the same way. He will come back in a cloud, and His foot is going to touch down on the Mount of Olives, and it's going to split wide open. He's going to walk right through that eastern gate and He's going to establish His reign and His rule from Jerusalem, the capital not only of the world, but of the universe (see Zechariah 14). He will reign there for a thousand years. He is now putting everything in place.

All of the Old Testament pointed to Jesus (the seed of woman) coming in a human body, God incarnate, to tabernacle with men. Jesus in the body of a baby, so that man might behold His glory, so they could see Him walking with them. God, in all of His glory: touching them, healing them, feeding them,

> Jesus ascended into a cloud. And what did the angels say to the followers? "Don't stand here gawking at the sky. You've got things to do."
> —Author's paraphrase

walking with them, sleeping with them, eating with them. They beheld His glory! They watched Him. When He left, what did He say? "It's better for you if I go, because here you just have Me, but if I go, I'll send My Spirit, and He won't just be with you; He will be in you" (John 16:7, paraphrased; see also 7:38–39; 14:26).

We have seen throughout Scripture that God has made His presence evident through the fire and the cloud. On the day of Pentecost, in Acts 2, God didn't want there to be any confusion about what was taking place. When He sent His Spirit, flames of fire were evident on every individual head. Why is that important? Because it all points back to everything He had been telling them would happen. All of Scripture has been pointing to God coming to indwell His people. He is saying, "I am here."

> Our earthly tents are now houses of the holy presence of God. How amazing is that? Do we—can we—grasp that?

What happened after those in the Upper Room were filled with that fiery Presence, with the Spirit of the living God? They began to proclaim the gospel boldly, without fear. Those who had been cowering and hiding and praying for ten days, waiting for God to do something, were suddenly filled with the Holy Spirit of God! They were filled with power and boldness, and they went out proclaiming the gospel in languages they didn't even know how to speak. God took over their physical bodies, and He was allowing everybody there to experience His manifestation.

This was Pentecost. Jews had come from everywhere to celebrate. In fact, I heard one person describe it as the kind of crowd you see at the mall on the day after Thanksgiving. That would be what the temple area crowd looked like on the day of Pentecost.

Everybody had come in. They were all hearing the disciples speak the gospel, the good news of Jesus Christ, in their own languages and even their own dialects. And they were blown away. They were pierced to the heart.

Peter stood up to preach, and three thousand people were saved. And those three thousand then got that same flame that we read about in Acts 2. And the day you called on Jesus Christ, that same flame came down into you, and He now lives within you. Our earthly tents are now houses of the holy presence of God. How amazing is that? Do we—can we—grasp that? Can we begin to wrap our little finite minds around such a lofty concept? I don't know that I can.

Jesus said, "Whoever believes in Me will be able to do what I have done, but they will do even greater things, because I will return to be with the Father" (John 14:12). If you read through the book of Acts, you are going to see some great things happen. Should we, as twenty-first-century Christians, not step back and ask, "Lord, does the modern-day church look like the church in Acts?" If it doesn't, it isn't His fault; it's ours.

What must I do to line my life up with God's Word in such a way that His Spirit is free to flow through me and do extraordinary things? Only when my life is in tune with His Spirit can I ask Him to fill me with power and boldness to speak the gospel, so I can see people saved and brought into the kingdom. Once people enter the kingdom of God, it becomes my responsibility and the responsibility of the church to "disciple them. *Form them in the practices and postures that* I have taught you," Jesus commanded, "and show them how to follow the commands I have laid down for you" (Matt. 28:20).

He promised that as we open His Word, His Spirit would teach us everything we need to know. Suddenly, not only am I going to see His presence all over the Word of God, but I will also see how all of Scripture points to Jesus Christ. Other themes, or threads, if you will, of God's character will start jumping up, coming to the surface, as we read the Word of God. You are going to see things through the revelation of His Spirit that you've never seen before.

And you know what? That's not just knowledge—that is revelation! You can't just casually read the Word of God and get that. It takes the Holy Spirit. He's the One who illumines it. He's the One who opens our eyes so that we can see, so that we comprehend and know the things only available to those who have His Spirit.

N. T. Wright says, "Heaven and earth are the two halves of God's created reality. Heaven is God's dimension; and earth is ours. From the ascension onward, the story of Jesus' followers takes place in both dimensions"[1]

The coming of the Holy Spirit and the establishment of the church were both based on the resurrection of Jesus Christ. Luke described Christ's resurrection appearances to His followers. Jesus was very much alive—even more so than they were. His disciples recognized Him. He ate with them. He conversed with them. He even told Thomas, "Touch Me and see; touch My scars and see that it's really Me."

But He also appeared and disappeared without going through doors. So He was different even though He was the same. The glorified bodies that we will receive one day will be at home in the physical realm, in the new heaven and new earth, and also at home in the spirit realm. The two will intersect, to be fully enjoyed and experienced forever. God is no longer just with us, but in us.

In Tim Keller's book *The Prodigal God*, he assures us of the reality of what God is preparing for those who know Him. "Jesus, unlike the founder of any other major faith, holds out hope for ordinary human life. Our future is not an ethereal, impersonal form of consciousness. We will not float through the air, but rather will eat, embrace, sing, laugh, and dance in the kingdom of God, in degrees of power, glory, and joy that we can't at present imagine."[2]

This life is temporary. Our earthly tents groan along with all of creation for the fulfillment of what everything we've been studying points to. We know there is more to come, and we long for it. Right now we live in parallel realms of reality: the physical realm and the spiritual realm. When we become believers, the two intersect, and there are times when God allows us to be very aware of the spirit realm. There is a way for us to walk in the physical realm while experiencing the reality of the eternal.

> "[We] will eat, embrace, sing, laugh, and dance in the kingdom of God, in degrees of power, glory, and joy that we can't at present imagine."
>
> –Tim Keller

There are times in your personal walk with God when you're reading the Word and a verse seems to jump off the page. You are very aware that this is not just a random thought, but one through which the Holy Spirit is revealing truth to you. Your heightened awareness enables you to understand that this is a moment when *the eternal is piercing the temporal*, and the Holy Spirit is speaking to you. And you know that. In your inner man, you know it.

Again, in our temporal state, we live in parallel realms of reality; however, we don't fully experience the eternal. But when we are like Christ, which Scripture is very clear we will be in our glorified bodies, we will be just as He was and is—perfectly at home in both realms.

Unfortunately, most Christians walk around in whatever reality or circumstances they find themselves in. Most are totally unaware that there is so much more for them to experience. They are vaguely aware of the longing in their hearts, but totally oblivious to the fact that it was placed there by God. He is constantly wooing and inviting us into that *unseen* reality. He set eternity in our hearts (Eccl. 3:11) so we would long for Him and the relationship we lost in Eden.

> What happened when Jesus cried out on that cross, "It is finished"? The veil in the temple was torn from top to bottom. There was no longer a need for the temple.

We need to understand something about heaven (the unseen reality). It is not light-years away from us. Heaven is all around us. In Scripture, when somebody is given a glimpse into the throne room, or into heaven, he or she is not necessarily transported anywhere.

Moses and the elders of Israel were sitting, having a meal on the mountaintop, and God allowed them to look at His footstool and see that the pavement of the throne room was as sapphire. They saw His presence, the glory of the Lord was in their midst, and yet He didn't consume them (Ex. 24:9–11).

When Isaiah experienced the beauty of the throne room, it was as if God opened a window or door (Isa. 6). Remember Elisha, when the army came against him, and his servant went outside? The servant saw the army and said, "Whoa! We're in trouble. They sent the entire army to get you!"

What did Elisha do? He said, "Do not fear, for those who are with us are more than those who are with them." Then he prayed, "Lord, open his eyes that he may see." Suddenly his servant saw the angelic chariots of fire. He was able to see what was already there—the veil was removed. The angelic chariots of fire all around protected them, and then God struck the army blind. Elisha led the blinded army to the king, and God granted them victory over their enemies (2 Kings 6).

When Paul experienced the spirit realm, he said he was taken to the third heaven (2 Cor. 12:2). There is a physical reality of the three heavens and there's a spiritual reality of them. In our physical understanding, there's the atmosphere around the earth, which is where Satan is confined until the end of time, until he's judged (Isa. 14:12; Eph. 2:2). Then there's the universe, which is the second heaven (Ps. 19:1). And then there's God's dwelling place, which is the third heaven (2 Cor. 12:2–4).

Yes, the heavens are like that, and yet at the same time, they're not—because there are two realms of reality that coexist. Our problem is that we are so bound to the physical and so often unaware of the spiritual. Yet it is just as real, and I often like to say it's *more* real than the physical, temporal realm that we're bound to right now. This entire temporal realm is passing away, but the spirit realm is eternal.

When we open the book of Revelation, we see that John is given wisdom and insight into what's actually happening in the presence of God. "I saw a door standing open in heaven . . ." (Rev. 4:1).

Do you understand the reason we can enter in and we can even see these things? It is because of Jesus Christ! What happened when He cried out on that cross, "It is finished"? The veil in the temple was torn from top to bottom. There was no longer a need for the temple. That's why God allowed the temple to be destroyed in AD 70. Jesus had completed everything the temple had pointed to.

Christ granted John the vision of the open door, and he was able to see. He said, "[I] heard [a] voice that sounded like a trumpet. "Come up here, and I will show you what must happen after this" (Rev. 4:1). God gave John a glimpse into heaven and the future so that he might have an understanding of end-time events.

Now listen to John's description of heaven:

I saw a throne that stood in heaven and One seated on the throne. The One enthroned gleamed like jasper and carnelian, and a rainbow encircled the throne with an emerald glow. Encircling that *great* throne were twenty-four *smaller* thrones with twenty-four elders clothed in white robes with wreaths fashioned of gold on their heads. Out of the *great* throne came flashes of lightning, sounds of voices, and peals of thunder. In front of the great throne, seven torches were ablaze, which are the seven Spirits of God. Also in front of the throne was a glassy sea of shimmering crystal.

In the midst of the throne and encircling the throne were four living creatures, covered all over with eyes, front to back. The first living creature was like a lion, the second creature was like an ox, the third creature had a face like the face of a human, and the fourth creature was like an eagle in full flight. These four living creatures, each of which had six wings and was covered with eyes—eyes on the outside and on the inside— did not cease chanting. All day and night *they were singing*.

Four Living Creatures:

"Holy, holy, holy
Is the Lord God who is the All Powerful,
who was, and who is, and who is coming.

And when the living creatures declared glory and honor and thanksgiving to the One seated on the throne, the One who lives throughout all the ages, the twenty-four elders fell prostrate before the One seated on the throne, worshiped the One who lives throughout all the ages, cast their *golden* wreaths before the throne, and chanted to *Him*.

24 Elders:

> Worthy are You, O Lord; worthy are You, O God,
>> to receive glory and honor and power.
> You *alone* created all things,
>> and through Your will *and by Your design,* they exist and
>>> were created.

(Rev. 4:2–11)

A door is opened, and John sees. Now think with me. Where is the throne? It is in the center. The twenty-four smaller thrones are around it. God's throne is the center of all that is happening.

Where was the tabernacle, in Old Testament times? It was in the center of the encampment. The Levites and all the other tribes of Israel were told where they were to camp around the tabernacle. The tabernacle was the center from which everything else was arranged.

And where is the Spirit of the living God now? He is in the center of my being—in my inner man. All of my life is to radiate out from that center where Christ dwells.

This understanding helps us when we want to hear from God. We must turn to His Word, and turn inward to His Spirit. Not out to the world. Not out to somebody else, unless he or she is a wise and godly counselor whom you trust.

We are to go to God's Word. We are to pray with one another to seek answers from the Lord. Turn inward to the Spirit of God who lives within you, and make sure He is on the throne of your life. Don't ever push Him off that throne; don't allow another person, a relationship, a desire, or even yourself to be on that throne. Make sure Jesus Christ is on the throne of your heart, that He is the center of your being, from which everything else flows. That is why the Word tells us, "Above all else, guard your heart, for every-thing you do flows from it" (Prov. 4:23 NIV).

God also gave John a vision of the new heaven and the new earth. In Revelation 21:2–7, John says:

> And I saw the holy city, the new Jerusalem, descending out of heaven from God, prepared like a bride *on her wedding day*, adorned for her husband *and for His eyes only*. And I heard a great voice, coming from the throne.

> **A Voice:**
>> See, the home of God is with *His* people.
>> He will live among them;
>> They will be His people,
>> And God Himself will be with them.
>> *The prophecies are fulfilled:*
>> He will wipe away every tear from their eyes.
>> Death will be no more;
>> Mourning no more, crying no more, pain no more,
>> For the first things have gone away.

> And the One who sat on the throne announced *to His creation*,

> **The One:** See, I am making all things new. (turning to me) Write *what you hear and see*, for these words are faithful and true. It is done! I am the Alpha and the Omega, the beginning and the end. I will see to it that the thirsty drink freely from the fountain of the water of life. To the victors will go this inheritance: I will be their God, and they will be My children.

The New Jerusalem is described as a bride, but is actually a city. It is fifteen hundred miles long, fifteen hundred miles wide, and fifteen hundred miles high. It is a cube, and it is adorned for the Lord. Why? Because it is the place where God dwells, and it will be the place where we dwell.

There's only one other cube mentioned in all of Scripture. Do you know what it is? The Holy of Holies! The New Jerusalem is the Holy of Holies of the universe, and that is where we're going to live forever.

Revelation 21:22–23 says, "And in the city, I found no temple because the Lord God, the All Powerful, and the Lamb are the temple. And in the city, there is no need for the sun to light *the day* or moon *the night* because the resplendent glory of the Lord provides the city with *warm, beautiful* light and the Lamb illumines every corner *of the new Jerusalem.*"

Revelation 22:4 tells us that we will see His face. We can't see His face right now because the full blaze of His holiness would consume us in our mortal, sinful flesh. But this tent is longing for that day when mortality is swallowed up in immortality, the finite becomes like God, and we will be like the resurrected Christ. Scripture tells us that we're going to be just like Him. And on that day, I will see His face, and you will too, if you know Jesus. Your eyes will see His face!

And we will dwell with God—in His presence, which is the Holy of Holies that will encompass all of the new creation. "The new heavens and earth are described as a temple because God's goal of universally expanding the temple of his glorious presence will have come to pass. Everything of which Old Testament temples were typologically

> "The new heavens and earth are described as a temple because God's goal of universally expanding the temple of his glorious presence will have come to pass."
>
> —G. K. Beale

symbolic, a recapitulated and escalated Garden of Eden and whole cosmos, will have finally been materialized."[3]

We currently struggle to see and comprehend spiritual truths. First Corinthians 13:12 says, "For now we see in a mirror dimly, but then face to face; now I know in part, but then I will know fully just as I also have been fully known" (NASB).

A few years ago, the Lord spoke to me very clearly at the home-going celebration of a precious woman of God. I was reflecting on what it is like to pass from the temporal and physical into the spiritual and eternal. Unexpectedly, I "saw" that when you die, God just opens the door and you step in. You enter His unveiled presence. That's all death is—a stepping through from the physical realm to the spiritual realm.

Jesus conquered death, hell, and the grave. He took the sting out. We don't have to fear death anymore. All of a sudden in my mind's eye, the Lord took me to the full-length mirror that stands in the corner of our bedroom. First Corinthians 13:12 came to my mind, and I saw myself standing before that mirror, straining to see. I jotted these words down on the funeral program:

Right now we see as in a mirror dimly,
Trying so hard to see more clearly.
Yet, all we see now are simply shadows of the true.
But one day, sweet friends, we're stepping through.
Then we will know fully as we have been known,
And yes, dear child of God, you will finally be home!

Jesus is who we're longing for. Nothing in this world will satisfy—only Jesus! And one day, we're going to see His face!

QUESTIONS TO CONSIDER

1. Colossians 3:4 states, "On that day when the Anointed One—who is our very life—is revealed, you will be revealed with Him in glory!" Is Christ your life?

2. Think about what it will be like to step from this life into the next. Are you ready to see His face?

NOTES

PART THREE

PRAYING THROUGH THE TABERNACLE

MINISTERING TO THE LORD IN THE TABERNACLE NOT MADE WITH HUMAN HANDS

As we have looked at the story behind the tabernacle, we have seen that it is our story, the story of all human beings—sinful, and in desperate need of a Savior. We have examined the furnishings of the tabernacle, seeing how each one can point us to Christ. Now, let us enter the tabernacle again, and this time consciously use each item to remind and inspire us as we minister to the Lord in prayer.

CHAPTER FIFTEEN

THE ALTAR

ABANDONING AND CONSECRATING

When the anointed One arrived as
High Priest of the good things that
are to come, *He entered* through a
greater and more perfect sanctuary
that was not part of the earthly
creation or made by human hands.

–Hebrews 9:11

When God calls a man, He
bids him come and die.

–Dietrich Bonhoeffer[1]

Tracing the presence of God through Scripture grants us a
clearer understanding of the significance of the tabernacle. Using
the tabernacle as a guide has greatly enhanced my personal time
with the Lord. It has also given me a greater sense of awe and reverence, as I understand the significance of being granted bold access
to the very throne of God.

Hebrews 4:16 tells us that when we pray, we are coming before that throne, the mercy seat of heaven. God said, "I will meet with you there. I will speak to you from above the seat of mercy" (Ex. 25:22). Come with a sense of expectation and ask the Lord to grant you "ears to hear" what He is saying.

We have been made a kingdom of priests (1 Peter 2:5, 9). We are now able to minister to the Lord just as the priests of old were consecrated to do (Lev. 7:35; Deut. 10:8). Do you understand that your time with the Lord is an opportunity for you not just to be ministered to, but to minister to the Lord? I still struggle trying to grasp the fact that the Holy One allows me to minister to Him!

Just as the tabernacle had three sections, we are a trichotomy—"spirit, soul, and body" (1 Thess. 5:23). Our spirits (the innermost part of our being) are now the Holy of Holies. The New Testament teaches that, as believers, we are temples of the Holy Spirit (1 Cor. 6:19–20). Our very bodies are to be houses of prayer because the Lord's presence is now within us.

Many people struggle trying to have a meaningful quiet time. Christians have heard people talk and teach about it, and they know they should spend time with the Lord, but so often they become frustrated and give up. We long to know God, but are often thwarted by our own flesh and the enemy.

I would like to invite you to walk with me through the tabernacle as we use the articles to direct our ministry to the Lord. I want to encourage you to have a special place and time that you meet with the Lord. Just as the tabernacle and then the temple became special places where God's manifest presence was experienced, your special place will become holy as well. You will begin to anticipate meeting with God, and His presence will beckon you to leave the ordinary trappings of this world and enter into His extraordinary presence.

The psalmist rightly said, "In Your presence is fullness of joy; at Your right hand are pleasures forevermore" (Ps. 16:11 NKJV). If you will make Christ your first love, He will satisfy your inner longings. He is the Friend that sticks closer than a brother. He has promised that He will never leave you or forsake you.

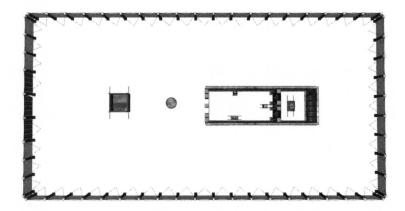

Look at the diagram above. You can use it as a pattern or guide for your personal time with the Lord. Remember, when you pray, you are coming before the very throne of the universe. God has welcomed you through His Son. You are clothed in His righteousness, not your sin. Your past no longer defines you. Christ has made you His, and you are "in Christ" (Eph. 1:3–4 NKJV).

As you enter your time with the Lord, stop at the brazen altar—the cross (Rom. 12:1). It is here that I offer myself as a living sacrifice—to be totally consumed. A living sacrifice was a burnt offering. The entire offering was consumed on the altar; nothing was left over, nothing held back. Death to the flesh must take place before I am able to hear and operate in the Spirit.

God lit the fire on the altar to consume the original sacrifices in Leviticus 9:24. He also lit the fire on the brazen altar of the temple (2 Chron. 7:1). But the priests were responsible to keep the fire going (Lev. 6:12–13). God lit the fire in our hearts at salvation. It is our responsibility to fan the flame through Bible study, prayer, fellowship with other believers, and serving according to our giftedness.

> "We have to know someone before we can truly love them. In order to know God, we must think about Him often."
>
> –Brother Lawrence

As we offer ourselves, we are to be consumed with and for Christ. Is this consumption not what Christ called us to when He said the greatest commandment was to "love the LORD your God with all your heart, all your soul, all your mind, and all your strength" (Mark 12:30 NLT)? That is an all-consuming love—with every fiber of your being.

How do you know what you love most—what you are consumed with? What do you think about in your free time? To what or whom does your mind automatically go when you are not occupied with something else? That thing, plan, project, relationship, or ministry has your heart—and that is idolatry.

We cannot be consumed with love for Christ if we don't really know Him and spend very little time with Him. We are to be consumed with Him—not projects for Him, but Him!

Brother Lawrence, the great seventeenth-century author of *The Practice of the Presence of God*, said, "We have to know someone before we can truly love them. In order to know God, we must think about Him often. And once we get to know Him, we will think about Him even more often, because where our treasure is, there also is our heart!"[2]

When my husband and I started dating in college, we wanted to spend as much time as possible with each other. We fell in love rather quickly and longed for the day when we could be together every day. We were engaged for a year while I completed college. During those days, we would stay out on dates until our college's curfew. Then I would go to my dorm room and wait for Steve to call me so we could listen to each other breathe!

We were in love and consumed with being together. I often think of that time in our lives and believe that this is what Christ was talking about in His letter to the Ephesians when He reprimanded them for leaving their first love. His instructions to them were to repent: to go back and do the things they had done at first (Rev. 2:4–5).

Those instructions work for our relationship with Christ and also our marriages. Many of you know how beneficial it is to relive your courtship and early-married days. It seems to rekindle those same feelings of love and longing. As we remember what it was like when we were first saved, we can recapture some of the excitement and wonder of forgiveness and life realized in Christ.

Think back to the time when you were "born again." Jesus told Nicodemus in John 3 that we must be "born of the Spirit" to enter the kingdom of God (v. 5–6 NASB). When did you receive forgiveness and the gift of eternal life? Salvation is a life exchange. Here at the cross, leave your life and take up the life of Christ. We are to be living Christs.

I have been greatly challenged by George Barna's definition of a true disciple:

> The true disciple of Jesus Christ is someone who is completely sold out to Christianity. To determine whether you really are a disciple, the relevant question concerns your level of commitment: *To what are you absolutely, fanatically devoted?* Jesus did not minister, die, and rise from the dead merely to enlist fans. He gave everything He had to create a community of uncompromising zealots—raving, unequivocal, undeterable, no-holds-barred spiritual revolutionaries. He has no room for lukewarm followers.[3]

To be consumed with Christ, we must daily die to our flesh. Just as dead men have no feelings, or rights, they also have no agenda. We must abandon our plans to the Lord as well. Some of the things we view as interruptions are actually divine appointments set by God. Am I sensitive enough to His Spirit to accept His plan without frustration and angst? Am I resting in Him, the One who said, "Come to Me, all who are weary and heavy-laden, and I will give you rest . . . My yoke is easy and My burden is light" (Matt. 11:28, 30 NASB)? Does my life depict that kind of rest?

If I have surrendered my all to Him and made myself His bondservant, then I am content to do His will. Peace and rest will depict this contentment. We must have the attitude of Christ (Phil. 2:5–11) and choose humility. Christ chose to submit to the Father, and we are to follow His example.

At the cross, I confess my submission to Christ and my love for Him. I ask Him to empower me to love Him with all of my heart, soul, mind, and strength. I declare my desire to have my will enveloped by His. Jesus said, during His ministry on earth, that He only did what the Father told Him to do. Christ did not feed every hungry person, heal every sick person, deliver every demonized person, or raise every widow's son from the dead. But He was still able to come to the end of His earthly life and declare that He had done everything the Father had for Him to do.

Oh, that you and I would be able to stand before the Lord one day with the assurance that we had completed His plan for our lives. To do that, we must die to ourselves daily and take up our cross and follow Jesus (Luke 9:23).

I wrote this chapter sitting in a hotel room in Louisville, Kentucky, waiting for my daughter to be admitted to the hospital to give birth to her first child—a little girl. She is our fifth grandchild. As I went to the Lord that morning, my time at the altar was centered on releasing Allison and her baby girl to the Lord. I desired only His will and to be His ambassador as I ministered to my daughter and her husband and to the hospital personnel.

> **We must die to ourselves daily and take up our cross and follow Jesus (Luke 9:23).**

Hadley arrived safely at 11:47 p.m. on July 4, amid much excitement. Mom and baby are both doing well.

Releasing our loved ones to God's perfect will is sometimes a struggle. We have all experienced it. But I encourage you to wrestle through and release—He is faithful, and He alone can empower you to face whatever each day requires in the midst of His supernatural peace.

The only way I can be an accurate reflection of Christ is to die and leave that crucified flesh at the altar. Have you ever smelled burned flesh or singed hair? It isn't a pleasant aroma. For me to exude the aroma of Christ, all my flesh must be totally consumed on the altar so that nothing of the stench of death is left. I long to reflect Christ and release the pleasing aroma of His resurrection.

Only then am I able to imitate Christ and have His life manifest in and through me.

David prayed and asked the Lord, "Create in me a clean heart, O God; restore within me a sense of being brand new" (Ps. 51:10). To "create" means to make out of nothing.[4] God doesn't just fix us up. He creates us anew every day as we come to Him. Nothing can be raised to life unless it dies. Dying hurts—it isn't fun—but the resurrection life on the other side is!

Jesus said, "Unless a grain of wheat is planted in the ground and dies, it remains a solitary seed. But when it is planted, it produces in death a great harvest" (John 12:24). It is as we follow the example of Christ and voluntarily lay our lives down, that He is glorified and moves in an extraordinary fashion through us. Death to the flesh leads to resurrection life—life in the Spirit. Resurrection life is life with a plus—it is the abundant life Christ promised His followers. This life can only be experienced through a personal relationship with Christ.

Christ was our Passover Lamb offered once for all on the brazen altar of the cross. Remember, the Passover was instituted by God to protect His people from the judgment that was coming to the Egyptians. God protected His people by the blood of the lamb.

God told the Israelites, "The blood shall be a sign for you on the houses where you live; and when I see the blood I will pass over you, and no plague will befall you to destroy you when I strike the land of Egypt" (Ex. 12:13 NASB). The blood of the Passover lamb was all they needed to be protected from death—the blood did it all. No cleaning up of self was required—that would come at the laver. *Just as I am*, He accepts and cleanses me.

Before proceeding to the laver, or basin, I ask that God's kingdom would come and His will would be done this day in my life on earth as it is in heaven (Matt. 6:10). I also ask the Lord to prepare my heart to receive His Word and my ears to hear His Spirit. I encourage you to pause for a moment and do the same.

QUESTIONS TO CONSIDER

1. Read Luke 9:23. Reflect on what it means to deny yourself and take up your cross.

2. How will this death affect your walk with Christ?

   Your relationships?

   Your acceptance of God's plan?

3. If you don't already have a place to meet with the Lord, prepare one now. How have you prepared your place, and what time have you set to meet with the Lord?

This chapter and the ones that follow will each end with a prayer testimony. The women who submitted these stories are personal friends and prayer warriors. I hope you will be encouraged by the truths God has revealed to them through prayer.

PERSEVERENCE IN PRAYER
Dayna's Story

When I was in the sixth grade, my father encouraged me to memorize Jeremiah 33:3, "Call unto me, and I will answer thee, and show thee great and mighty things, which thou knowest not" (KJV). He then challenged me to begin praying for God to do big things in my life. As I memorized the verse, the truth of its promise made itself at home in my heart. I began to believe God would do things that were greater than I could imagine on my own. The diligent prayers of my parents on my behalf and my own fledgling "Belief 101" prayers began to craft the course of my life. Over the next few years, I saw God answer many prayers on my behalf, including the miraculous provision of a full scholarship to college and meeting the godly man who would become my soul mate, best friend, and husband.

Early in our marriage, I learned another powerful prayer principle from the pages of God's Word. Luke 18:1–8 records the parable Jesus told of the persistent widow and the unjust judge. The widow, with few legal rights, was dealing with someone who was trying to take advantage of her. Her only recourse was to appear before a judge who had no fear of God and no interest in the welfare of the poor woman. Undaunted by his lack of concern, she continued to show up in his courtroom to plead her case. Finally, just to get her out of his hair, he granted her request. Jesus utilized this parable to teach us to be persistent in our prayers. Sometimes, God answers our prayers immediately; at other times, we must persevere for months or even years before our petitions are granted.

One of those times of perseverance in prayer was regarding the salvation of my father-in-law. My husband came to know Christ when he was in college. One of the first people with whom he shared Christ after he was saved was his father. His father was a good man, but Bill knew his dad had never committed his life to Christ. His father either ignored or rejected Bill's attempts to share Christ with him over and over again. For twenty-five years, we prayed for his father to be saved, and Bill continued to share Christ with him at every opportunity. In July 2002, Bill was visiting with his parents in Nashville and asked his dad if he had been thinking about what they'd talked about the last time he was home. "What do you mean?" asked his dad. Bill replied, "Have you thought any more about where you will spend eternity?" His dad responded, "No, it makes me nervous to think about it." In a sovereign moment, Bill said, "Dad, it should make you nervous if you realize that if you die, you will spend an eternity in hell." A tear began to roll down his father's cheek. Bill was then able to share with his dad once again how to be saved, and his father prayed to receive Christ that day, at the age of eighty-four. A couple of weeks later, Bill went back and had the privilege of baptizing his father.

Earlier this year, Bill sat with his mother beside his father's bed as his dad breathed his last earthly breath and entered into eternal life in heaven at the age of ninety-five. When Bill preached his dad's funeral, it was a time of victory and celebration because his family knew without a doubt that his father was in the presence of Jesus. As far as Bill knows, there was only one other person besides himself who shared Christ with his father in the ninety-five years he walked on this earth. As I sat at the funeral that day, I kept thinking how different that day would have been if Bill had not persistently prayed and shared Christ with his father for all of those years.

As you believe God for great things and persevere in your prayers, you will find as I did that "prayer is the hand of God that turns promises into performance."[5]

NOTES

CHAPTER SIXTEEN

THE LAVER

CLEANSING AND REFLECTING

*. . . so that He might sanctify her,
having cleansed her by the washing
of water with the word.*

–Ephesians 5:26 (NASB)

After surrendering my will to the Father, I am ready to open His Word and allow His truth to open my eyes and pierce my heart. "All of Scripture is God-breathed; *in its* inspired *voice, we hear* useful teaching, rebuke, correction, *instruction, and* training for a life that is right" (2 Tim. 3:16). Here I wash myself in the laver of His Word. The laver, as you recall, was where the priests would cleanse their hands and feet. God's Word is the agent that cleanses us and renews our minds (Rom. 12:2). We are cleansed by the washing of the water of the Word (Eph. 5:26 NASB; see also 1 John 1:9; John 15:3).

At the altar, the blood was used for cleansing. At the laver, the water was used for cleansing. The blood cleanses from past sins, and the water of His Word cleanses from present ones. "The brazen altar grants access to God's righteousness and the laver to His holiness," says Betty Vick. "The blood effects our standing before God and the water affects our state or condition with God."[1]

As you pick up the Word of God and begin reading in your *One Year Bible* or other reading plan, consider the context and time period of the author or main characters. Remember that these were real, flesh-and-blood people. The most important question we can ask as we read is, "What is God revealing about Himself?" God systematically and progressively revealed Himself through the Bible. Oh, that we would never lose the wonder of our God and Creator revealing Himself to us!

It is so important that we make decisions and view life through the lens of Scripture. There is no other way to think sanely and accurately except as we align our thinking with God's Word. The world loses its moral bearings when life is viewed outside of God's Word. The "natural man" (1 Cor. 2:14 KJV) will self-destruct without the Lord. Our sin nature takes over, and we live according to our own reason. The broad path really does lead to destruction!

If you have a copy of the Word of God to read in your language, you are blessed indeed! I recently watched a video of a tribal people in Indonesia receiving the entire New Testament translated into their language. Before 2010, they only had portions of the Scripture in their language. They had prepared an ark-type carrier to transport the Bibles from the airstrip to their village. There was much crying and celebrating as they joyfully received God's Word. They were dancing and singing and praising God for His goodness.

It was so convicting to see how these people had longed for God's Word and now were celebrating God's goodness to provide it for them. I wept as I rejoiced and yet felt convicted that I did not open God's Word each morning with a sense of joy and wonder. I have multiple copies of the Bible in various translations and other study resources to aid in my understanding. How is it that I am so blessed and yet so often unaware and ungrateful?

I should enter my "secret place" with the Lord with great anticipation. The God of the universe, who resides within my physical body, desires to speak to me and change me through His Word. "Delight yourself in the LORD," says Psalm 37:4, "and He will give you the desires of your heart" (NASB). "Delight" comes from a "primitive root, to be soft."[2] As we delight in Him, He molds us into His image and His desires become our desires.

Matthew Henry stated, "To delight in God is as much a privilege as a duty. He has not promised to gratify the appetites of the body, and the humours of the fancy, but the desires of the renewed, sanctified soul. What is the desire of the heart of a good man? It is this, to know, and love, and serve God."[3] As we repose in Him, He changes our hearts to reflect His.

> "What is the desire of the heart of a good man? It is this, to know, and love, and serve God."
>
> —Matthew Henry

The Word of God is compared to a mirror in James 1:23–25. As we look intently into the Word of God, we see ourselves as we really are. Then the Word does its work as it corrects, instructs, rebukes, and teaches. But I must pause long enough to gaze *intently* into the perfect law of liberty, or I will miss what is so evident to the seeking eye and heart.

That is why it is so important to have a set *time*—an appointment with God each day. This appointment is truly the most important time of your day. I am not fit to go out into my day until my Master has instructed me. Every day I must die to my will and immerse myself in His.

God will use the Word to reveal even the thoughts and intents of my heart. "For the word of God is living and active and sharper than any two-edged sword, and piercing as far as the division of soul and spirit, of both joints and marrow, and able to judge the thoughts and intentions of the heart" (Heb. 4:12 NASB).

There are times when I am praying that I am made aware of an unkind or jealous thought. It may be a wrong motive that is exposed as I am praying about a certain request. God's Word is able to reveal and expose. But God does it in such a way that His "kindness . . . leads you to repentance" (Rom. 2:4 NASB). Condemnation and shame come from the enemy. God is gentle, and His goal is always repentance and restoration.

> Condemnation and shame come from the enemy. God is gentle, and His goal is always repentance and restoration.

Listen for His voice as you read His Word. If there is a verse that is especially meaningful, or seems to be in bold print, then you know the Lord is speaking to you. I would encourage you to write it on a three-by-five card and begin to meditate on it and possibly even memorize it. Knowing the Word and meditating on it will change the way you think.

My husband recently prepared a message for his series on the family. He was speaking on discipleship in the home. There had been much discussion that week on the news about the Supreme Court's decision on the Defense of Marriage Act and the striking down of a portion of Proposition 8 in the state of California. Gay rights advocates were celebrating a victory, and we were wondering what this would mean for

Christians and the church. We had discussed the responsibility of parents to train their children in the Scriptures and to prepare them for the world in which we live.

My husband left early for church, and I went to my chair to read my Bible and spend time with the Lord. As I opened my *One Year Chronological Bible* to that day's portion of scripture, I read from Isaiah. The following verses seemed to jump off the page:

> If you will not believe, you surely shall not last. . . . You are not to say, 'It is a conspiracy!' in regard to all that this people call a conspiracy, and you are not to fear what they fear or be in dread of it. It is the LORD of hosts whom you should regard as holy. And He shall be your fear, and He shall be your dread. Then He shall become a sanctuary. (Isa. 7:9; 8:12–14 NASB).

I texted my husband those words as an encouragement.

The news on every channel seems to sensationalize every story, and conspiracy theories abound! Yet, the Lord is the only one we are to revere or fear, and when we do, He will be our safe place.

In this world that doesn't acknowledge God or His Word, we must stand firm on what the Bible says. Our job is to believe! We can leave the judging to the Lord. You can be sure "the Judge of all the earth [will] do what is right" (Gen. 18:25 NLT). As Dietrich Bonhoeffer stated, "It is not our judgement of the situation which can show us what is wise, but only the truth of the Word of God. Here alone lies the promise of God's faithfulness and help. It will always be true that the wisest course for the disciple is always to abide solely by the Word of God in all simplicity."[4]

We are to abide in and to live by the Word of God. If my reason is contrary to the Word of God, then my reason is wrong. If the world doesn't understand, or thinks I am wrong or intolerant, that is all right. The world hated Christ, and He told us that just as it rejected Him, it would reject and hate His followers (Matt. 24:9; 27:18; John 15:18).

Allow the Word of God to instruct you and teach you. His Word is truth and is your very life!

∼ QUESTIONS TO CONSIDER ∼

1. Select a reading plan and make yourself accountable to your small group or an accountability partner. Read through the Bible every year. What plan have you committed to?

2. Start memorizing scripture. One verse per week is an achievable goal. The Navigators have an excellent tool that provides suggested scriptures to memorize that every Christian should know. It is called the Topical Memory System.[5] There is also a list of suggested scriptures to memorize in the appendix of this book. These are the scriptures that my discipleship groups memorize.

★ ★ ★

Read the following testimony and reflect on how God desires to speak to you through His Word and transform your prayer life.

NO DISTANCE
Pam's Story

Several years ago, while on a women's mission trip in Timisoara, Romania, a special moment of God's truth was sealed in my heart as a friend and I read scripture and prayed. Initially, the day had begun with disappointment when the group of women we were traveling with was separated into two groups. One group went on to carry out our mission of a women's conference for pastors' wives in Romania. My friend and I remained behind in the second group to wait for boxes of children's shoes to clear customs. We were going to give the shoes to children living in the small towns and villages where we would be ministering. We had talked and prayed so much for the pastors' wives prior to the trip that it took me more than a few moments to readjust to God's new itinerary.

My friend and I sat silently with our Bibles open in a large, empty room with a few chairs and a table. I began reading through Paul's letter to the Colossians. When I arrived at Colossians 2:5, Paul's words jumped off the page and into my heart. I was stunned by the truth that embraced my soul: "For though I am absent from you in body, I am present with you in spirit and delight to see how disciplined you are and how firm your faith in Christ is" (NIV).

God's awesome presence filled my heart, and He said clearly, *"There is* no distance *in the spiritual realm. My spirit lives in you and in all who have trusted Me. We are one body in Christ and eternally connected in spirit with each other."* In that moment, I realized that my friend and I were not physically at the pastors' wives conference, but our spirits were connected with our precious sisters in Christ. We were at the conference! By changing our plans, God had given us the awesome privilege of uninterrupted praying and conversing with Him as He revealed specific needs for our friends and the pastors' wives. The quietness and confidence of this "God moment" became my strength.

Since that time, God has brought full circle the truth of "no distance" in many areas of my life. I came to realize His presence in times of loneliness and separation: He was there in my early childhood when I cried myself to sleep feeling alone and abandoned. He was there when the tears came as my daughters went to college, lived in other countries, and moved to other states. He was there when friends moved away and I said good-bye through tears. He was there on the mission field when we said our tearful good-byes to our sisters and brothers around the world. And He was there most recently when I was diagnosed with multiple myeloma (blood cancer). The "no distance" prayers of family and friends continue to be life-giving reminders that I am not alone. I live in continuous gratitude of my Father's awesome presence, and for the gift of prayer that keeps me connected to Him and to others.

NOTES

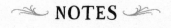

CHAPTER SEVENTEEN

THE LAMPSTAND

FILLING AND ILLUMINATING

*If we walk step by step in the light,
where the Father is, then we are
ultimately connected to each other
through the sacrifice of Jesus His Son.*

—1 John 1:7

After ministering to the Lord in the outer court, we move through the next gate to the Holy Place. Unfortunately, so many people never move beyond the outer court in their ministry to the Lord or in their spiritual life. Too many believers have stopped at the brazen altar of salvation but have never seriously applied the Word to their lives or grown beyond spiritual infancy. Remember that each level of the tabernacle had more restrictions, and fewer people were allowed to enter. Only those who seek God with their whole heart will experience the intimacy of the inner court.

Immersing our minds in the Word of God prepares us to move into the Holy Place and pause at the golden lampstand. This beautiful lampstand of pure hammered gold would catch the eye of the priest as he entered. The almond blossom cups and branches of the lampstand represent Christ in several ways. Christ is the central shaft or head of the church, as we have seen. He is also the Light of the World and of our paths. He fills us with His Holy Spirit, and He is for us the Tree of Life (Gen. 3:22).

> God lights the way ahead for us. He gives us just enough light to take the next step, to do the next thing.

We are first introduced to the Tree of Life in the garden of Eden. After sin entered the human race, God removed Adam and Eve from the garden so they would not eat from the Tree of Life and be forever lost in their sinful condition.

In Christ's letter to the church of Ephesus, we are told, "He who has an ear, let him hear what the Spirit says to the churches. To him who overcomes, I will grant to eat of the tree of life which is in the Paradise of God" (Rev. 2:7 NASB). *Paradise* literally means "an Eden, a place of future happiness."[1] This Eden will be the New Jerusalem, where we will dwell with God forever.

I was teaching through the Bible at a women's conference in New Delhi, India, when I saw this truth in a way I had never seen before. We had taught through the fourteen eras of Scripture, helping the women grasp the "big picture" of God's story.[2]

I was teaching on the last era, the end times, and I was reading Revelation 22, about the Tree of Life that will be on both sides of the river, "bearing twelve kinds of fruit, yielding its fruit every month; and the leaves of the tree were for the healing of the nations. There will no longer be any curse" (vv. 2–3 NASB). I shouted when I read this! Suddenly, I "saw" what I had only known before. There is only one tree in the New Jerusalem! There will no longer even be the temptation to sin! There is only one tree, and His name is Jesus Christ—He is the Tree of Life!

Just as life is found in Christ, there is no real light apart from Him. Darkness fills the earth, and natural light does not illumine our spirits. It takes the light of Christ to open our eyes and hearts to truth. Jesus was and is the Light of the World. He said, "I am the Light of the world; he who follows Me will not walk in the darkness, but will have the Light of life" (John 8:12 NASB).

Just as the lampstand lit the area in front of it, God lights the way ahead for us. He gives us just enough light to take the next step, to do the next thing. He has promised to meet all our needs if we will "seek first His kingdom and His righteousness" (Matt. 6:33 NASB). But we are to focus on the needs for today—not for tomorrow. Don't borrow trouble; each day has enough of its own (Matt. 6:34).

You may remember from chapter 8 that the lampstand was to be maintained by the priests every morning and evening. They were to keep it filled with oil and the wicks trimmed and burning. Their service is such a beautiful picture of our responsibility before the Lord to continually be filled with His Spirit and to be lights in our dark world.

The oil of the lampstand represents the Holy Spirit. Just as the lampstand was to be daily filled with oil, so we must be filled by the Holy Spirit (Eph. 5:18). We must ask the Lord through prayer to fill us with His Spirit. We receive this filling by grace through faith. Andrew Murray said in *Prayer Power,* "The connection between the prayer life and the Spirit life is close and indissoluble. It is not merely that we can receive the Spirit through prayer, but the Spirit life requires, as an indispensable thing, a continuous prayer life. I can be led continually by the Spirit only as I continually give myself to prayer."[3]

Calvin Miller said, "His filling gives me that glorious sense of 'life worth' once again. I believe that a lack of the spiritual disciplines always triggers this periodic emptiness. That is, when I quit making myself pray, study the Scripture, and minister in His name, I become depleted . . . All strength ultimately resides in the spiritual discipline."[4]

It does take discipline to "fix your eyes on Jesus" and apply His Word to your life. (See Hebrews 12:2 NASB.) You must be diligent to make time for prayer and ministry in His name. It is so easy to become busy and neglect the most important things.

Are you in Christ? Have you been born again? Are you filled with the Holy Spirit and allowing His light to shine through you? Pause now and ask the Lord to fill you with His Holy Spirit. Thank Him by faith for His filling and that you will one day partake of the Tree of Life in the paradise prepared for us by God.

QUESTIONS TO CONSIDER

1. How can you tell when you are filled by the Spirit? One of the primary evidences is the fruit of the Spirit being manifest in your life. Read and memorize Galatians 5:22–23.

2. Is your light shining "before men in such a way that they may see your good works, and glorify your Father who is in heaven" (Matt. 5:16 NASB)? How is God working in and through you?

3. We are to be serving in a local body of Christ according to the gifts God has given (1 Cor. 12–14). Are you an active member of a

local body of Christ? How are you operating in the gifting of the Holy Spirit? If you don't know what your spiritual gifts are, you can take a test at http://www.bellevue.org/sitefiles/1696/custom/gifts/giftsintro.htm. Scroll down the page and click on Spiritual Gifts Test. Once you have discovered your gifts put them to use in your local church.

 Read the following testimony. It reminds us that just as the lampstand was to keep burning and never go out, we must persevere in prayer and never give up!

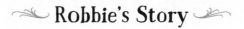

WHEN WE CAN'T SEE WHAT'S AHEAD
Robbie's Story

In September 2006, a beautiful baby girl named Alyssa came into our lives. Our family had known her mother, Rebekah, for many years. When Rebekah was four months pregnant with Alyssa, she came to live with us. I was in the delivery room when Alyssa was born and was the first person to hold her. A few days later, we brought them both home from the hospital to live with us. They lived in our home for one year, and then Rebekah decided to take Alyssa and move into an apartment on her own. During the following year, Rebekah had a back injury and, as a result, she became addicted to prescription medication. Her life took a fast downward spiral. Our family prayed for two years for Rebekah's life to turn around without seeing any change.

In January 2010, my husband, Bruce, and I received temporary custody of Alyssa. We continued to pray that Rebekah would become the mother and woman the Lord had purposed for her life. However, it seemed our prayers would again be unanswered. On June 3, 2010, we received a phone call that Rebekah had died of an accidental overdose.

We sought God's directions, and then Bruce and I immediately petitioned the court to adopt Alyssa. At that point, Alyssa's birth father entered into the picture and opposed our petition. Prior to this time, Alyssa had only seen him three times in her life.

For three long years since we filed our petition, we have been praying for the Lord to allow us to adopt Alyssa and make her fully and legally our daughter. And until now, we have not received an answer to this prayer! Alyssa will be seven years old this year, and in our own human understanding, we believe she needs permanence. In spite of all of this, we know our Lord to be faithful and trustworthy, and we know that "all things . . . work together for good to those who love God" (Rom. 8:28 NASB). So we will . . . continue in prayer!

NOTES

CHAPTER EIGHTEEN

THE TABLE OF SHOWBREAD

STRENGTHENING AND SATISFYING

On the same night the Lord Jesus was betrayed, He took the bread *in His hands*; and after giving thanks *to God*, He broke it and said, "This is My body, *broken* for you. Keep doing this so that you *and all who come after* will have a vivid reminder of Me."

–I Corinthians 11:23–24

The soul is dangerously anorexic when it doesn't have a daily appetite for Christ.

–Ann Voskamp[1]

After pausing at the lampstand and being filled with the Spirit, we move to the table of showbread. It is here that we partake of Jesus, who is the Bread of Life (John 6:35, 48). He alone can satisfy and feed the hungry and thirsty places in our souls. He also strengthens us in our inner man (Eph. 3:16) and enables us to fulfill the task to which He has called us.

I would encourage you as you reflect upon Christ to thank the Father for all He has provided through His Son. It is very beneficial to praise Jesus through the names used for Him in the Bible. He is:

- the gate to the sheepfold
- the sacrificial Lamb slain for my sin
- the Word who cleanses
- the Word who reveals
- the Light of the World
- the Spirit who fills and satisfies
- the Bread of heaven that nourishes and strengthens me
- my Intercessor
- my Advocate before the Father
- the Veil that was torn
- the atonement blood on the mercy seat
- Savior
- Lord
- Master
- Son of God
- Son of man
- Bridegroom
- a sure foundation
- a faithful friend
- Healer
- hope
- Truth
- King of kings and Lord of lords
- the Great I AM[2]

This list is only a sample of His names. Sylvia Gunter encourages people to make their own list of the names and attributes of God as a "personal affirmation that He is more than adequate as your Need-meeter. God is a covenant-keeping God. He is covenantally committed to being true to His names and attributes by which He has revealed Himself to His people."[3]

Jesus Christ is the Bread from God that we cannot live without. He provides spiritual sustenance to those who seek Him. He is the answer to your every need.

When Christ was tempted in the wilderness, He responded to the devil after the first temptation with Deuteronomy 8:3: "What makes you truly alive is not the bread you eat but following every word that comes from the mouth of the Eternal One." Physical bread alone cannot sustain us; we must partake of Christ—the Bread of heaven.

The table of showbread had a rim around it to prevent the bread from falling off. This rim is a beautiful picture of the protection we enjoy because we are "in Christ." The table of showbread can be seen as a picture of "the people of God—carried by Christ, hemmed in and protected by Him."[4]

We have already seen that the table is a place of communion with Christ and others. Here we commune with Him just as He invited the church at Laodicea to do. Christ said, "Look! I stand at the door and knock. If you hear my voice and open the door, I will come in, and we will share a meal together as friends" (Rev. 3:20 NLT).

> Christ said, "Look! I stand at the door and knock. If you hear my voice and open the door, I will come in, and we will share a meal together as friends" (Rev. 3:20 NLT).

This past spring I was scheduled to speak at a women's conference. I was planning to drive since it was only about an hour and a half away. I look forward to time alone in the car because it gives me extended times of communion with the Lord. I was praying as

I drove and reflecting on the scripture through which the Lord had been speaking to me recently.

I was walking back through John 5–6 in my mind. Jesus had healed a paralytic, been confronted by the religious elite, and then had left for the Sea of Galilee. There a large crowd gathered to hear Him teach. He taught them, and then He had them sit down. After blessing a little boy's lunch, Jesus fed the five thousand. Then He sent the disciples away in a boat, and He went up on the mountain by Himself to pray.

A storm arose on the sea, and the disciples were straining at the oars. During the fourth watch (between 3 and 6 a.m.), Jesus came walking on the water. The gospel of Matthew also records this incident and tells us that Peter called out to Him, "Lord, if it is You, command me to come to You on the water" (Matt. 14:28 NASB). Jesus did, and Peter stepped out of the boat and walked on water! This is a physical impossibility! Yet, Peter was walking on water—until he took his eyes off Jesus and looked at the waves. Immediately fear filled his heart, and he began to sink.

Peter cried out to Jesus, who took him by the hand and stepped into the boat with him. Jesus rebuked him for his lack of faith. Immediately the wind stopped, and they were on the other side of the Sea of Galilee. Wow! What an experience!

As I thought about Peter, I realized that faith and fear cannot coexist in the human heart. The moment I take my eyes off Jesus, fear will crowd out faith, and I, too, will begin to sink below my

> Faith and fear cannot coexist in the human heart. The moment I take my eyes off Jesus, fear will crowd out faith, and I will begin to sink below my circumstances.

circumstances. The only way to walk above the storms in our lives is to "[fix] our eyes on Jesus" (Heb. 12:2 NASB).

The crowd from the day before came looking for Jesus and wanted to know how He had gotten to the other side. Jesus told them they had only followed Him because He had fed them. He then told them not to work for food that perishes, but to work for the food that endures to eternal life. When they asked Jesus what they should do to do the works of God, He responded, "This is the work of God, that you *believe* in Him whom He has sent" (John 6:29 NASB; emphasis added). Our job is to believe!

I began to praise the Lord that He is Lord over nature and over all of my circumstances. Suddenly, I remembered the new CD I had downloaded but hadn't yet listened to. Wanting to worship the Lord with song, I began listening and skipping through the beginning of each song. I stopped on one that nearly took my breath. The words were almost identical to what the Lord had been speaking to my heart. Isn't it amazing how the Lord speaks to us through various mediums when our hearts are open to His voice?

A. W. Tozer said in *The Pursuit of God*, "The facts are that God is not silent, has never been silent. It is the nature of God to speak. The second Person of the Holy Trinity is called the Word."[5]

As you can imagine, tears began to stream, my hands went up in the air, and I was driving with my knee! This is communion! These moments of transcendence are what you live for! Christ in you, communing and strengthening and instructing you through the presence of His Spirit! Needless to say, I was filled and full of joy when I arrived at the women's conference.

Our job is to believe. As we believe and choose to walk by faith, we can't help but reflect on all that Christ has done for us. Partake of the Bread of heaven and allow Him to feed you with food that the world knows nothing about.

Oh, what our Savior sacrificed that we might enter in! Do not hesitate to partake. There are spiritual treasures for the asking.

QUESTIONS TO CONSIDER

1. When was the last time you experienced the manifest presence of God?

2. One way to partake of the living Word is to meditate upon it and memorize it. Choose a verse through which the Lord has spoken to you, and commit it to memory.

Read the following testimony. Jesus is sufficient for your every need!

TRANSFORMING THE MOUNTAIN OF FEAR
Patti's Story

Our second child was born without the left side of her heart. We were told that she would need two experimental surgeries that were only done in one place, thousands of miles away, and those surgeries would be grueling and life threatening. The statistics were not in our favor.

The first surgery was just what doctors had said it would be. They couldn't tell us exactly when the second surgery would happen, but somewhere around the time our daughter turned two years old. After spending months of recovery in that faraway hospital, I knew what we didn't want. We did not want unscheduled "fix-it" surgeries. Those never went well. We had already watched too many of our new heart friends lose their babies during "repairs." Our little family survived surgery and made it home, but we were barely functioning because my eyes were fixed on the "what-ifs."

I was sleep deprived and under great oppression and fear. Even when I laid my head down for much-needed sleep, my dreams betrayed me and nightmares stole my rest. When I saw what was happening to me in that dark night of life, it scared me to my very core. It got so bad that in one pivotal moment, I cried out in desperation, and my cry was literal. "Whatever it takes, Lord . . . do whatever it takes to get me out of this! Release me from this fear and depression."

And He answered, not in the way I had imagined, but in the way I most needed. Suddenly, we were back on a plane, headed for a "fix-it" repair. I felt like Abraham walking up the mountain with my child . . . Would God require a sacrifice of me? Would the outcome be the same? This unplanned surgery was not just a fearful thing . . . He had brought me to the feet of my *greatest* fear. I cried out again, this time for the strength to keep moving up that towering peak. His presence helped me transform that mountain of fear into an offering.

With one sweep of His great right hand, the surgery was over. We were home. He had brought me to the feet of my greatest fear . . . and there? *There* . . . He showed me He was God; the great I AM; Savior; Redeemer; God over all things; God over all people; God over ALL! And especially, God over my child, who is, today, a pediatric cardiology nurse.

NOTES

CHAPTER NINETEEN

THE ALTAR OF INCENSE

ABIDING AND INTERCEDING

We have an Advocate with the Father,
Jesus Christ the righteous.

—1 John 2:1 (NASB)

There is no power like that of prevailing
prayer—of Abraham pleading for Sodom,
Jacob wrestling in the stillness of the
night, Moses standing in the breach,
Hannah intoxicated with sorrow, David
heartbroken with remorse and grief, Jesus
in sweat and blood . . . such prayer prevails.

—Samuel Chadwick[1]

The altar of incense was before the veil that separated the Holy Place from the Holy of Holies. The veil has been torn, so there is no longer a separation between God's manifest presence and the redeemed. This altar represents the golden bowls before the throne, where our prayers are held (Rev. 5:8). The fire that lit the incense on this altar was taken from the fire of the burnt offering (brazen altar). The prayers we offer are only a pleasing aroma when uttered by lips speaking from the heart of a living sacrifice (Psalm 141:2; Romans 12:1; Revelation 8:3). This "burning heart" has been ignited by the fire that God started (Lev. 9:24).

For the believer this fire is ignited at salvation, but must be maintained by wholehearted devotion to the Lord. "Blessed are the pure in heart," Jesus said, "for they shall see God" (Matt. 5:8 NASB). Diligently guard your heart from lesser things and pursuits. Christ alone is worthy! As He becomes your heart's desire, your every desire will be satisfied in Him.

Follow Christ's example. "When Jesus was *on the earth, a man of* flesh *and blood*, He offered up prayers and pleas, groans and tears to the One who could save Him from death. He was heard because He approached God with reverence" (Heb. 5:7).

It is as we have prepared our hearts that we, too, will be heard, and we are now able to pray according to God's will. To ready our hearts we first stopped at the brazen altar and died to our own will and way. We next washed ourselves in the Word, confessing anything revealed by His Spirit. Then we made our way to the lampstand and asked the Lord to fill us with His Spirit and light the path that He has chosen for us. We enjoyed His fellowship as we spent time with Him and partook of Him at the table of showbread. Then we came before His throne to ascribe to Him all glory

> "If we would but teach our wandering brethren to simply believe and diligently pray, rather than engaging in endless reasonings, we would lead them sweetly into the arms of God."
>
> –Jeanne Guyon

and honor, thanksgiving and praise. Here we stand in the gap for the lost, intercede for those in need, and lay our petitions before His throne.

We make that trek to our chairs or special places each morning because we long to meet with God and hear from Him. We yearn for those times when the eternal pierces the temporal and we sense God's presence in an unmistakable and indescribable way. Those moments change us. The chains fall off. The sin that entangles loses its hold, and the soul's hunger is increased for more of Him and less of the world or self. It is here that we "turn [our] eyes upon Jesus. Look full in His wonderful face. And the things of earth will grow strangely dim in the light of His glory and grace."[2]

I have often teased that I have been discipled by "dead" people. One of those who still speaks (though she is with the Lord) is Jeanne Guyon. In her book, *Experiencing Union with God Through Prayer,* she said,

> The decay of internal holiness is unquestionably the source of many sins that have appeared in the world. All these would be overthrown if inward devotion were reestablished. Sin takes possession of the soul deficient in faith and prayer. If we would but teach our wandering brethren to simply believe and diligently pray, rather than engaging in endless reasonings, we would lead them sweetly into the arms of God."[3]

It is basking in the love and acceptance of God that propels us onward and upward in our Christian journey. Duty alone will never sustain us. Oh, if only we would spend time in His presence, and allow intimacy with Christ to gratify and make us glad! Spending time with Christ in prayer awakens our love and causes us to "greatly rejoice with joy inexpressible and full of glory" (1 Peter 1:8 NASB). When is the last time you experienced this kind of joy?

Through prayer we are able to fix our eyes on Jesus (Heb. 12:1–2) and run the race that He has set before us. We are also able to stand against the schemes of the evil one. We live in hostile territory with a very real enemy. The only way we can make it without becoming a casualty is to listen to and follow our Savior.

In the same way that the Hebrews could fight the battles of the promised land only after they had learned to worship, we too must truly worship in order to be equipped to fight the daily battles of this broken planet. The preparation we have made as we have gotten our hearts ready for prayer enables us to enter into the battle for humankind. Remember that prayer is not preparation for the battle—it is the battle!

> "The Holy Spirit wants us to know that God is not some fast-food supplier of our 'McPrayerlife.' He is the unhurried Jehovah who treasures those wonderful moments of leisure that we freely give Him."
>
> —Calvin Miller

One morning as I was reading through my *One Year Bible*, the assigned portion of Scripture was in Deuteronomy. Suddenly, Deuteronomy 13:4 seemed to jump off the page. I knew that the Lord was speaking to me through this verse. I took out a three-by-five-inch card and wrote down the verse. Then I took out my *Strong's Exhaustive Concordance* and looked up the six verbs in the verse.

As I meditated on these words, it seemed as though they contained a progression—a sequence of action that would lead to victory: "You shall **follow** the LORD your God and **fear** Him; and you shall **keep** His commandments, **listen** to His voice, **serve** Him, and **cling** to Him" (Deut. 13:4 NASB; bold added for emphasis). Follow, fear, keep, listen, serve, and cling. As I *follow* Christ through salvation, and *fear* (revere) Him, I will *keep* His commandments. As I obey, I will be able to *hear* (listen with intent to obey) His voice and obey through *service* (worship) and *cling* to Him as He takes me safely home.

The picture I had in my mind was of a soldier crossing a minefield. The enemy has set traps for us. Christ is omniscient (all-knowing) and as I cling to Him, He will navigate the minefield and take me safely to the other side.

My heart was full as I marveled at all the Lord had revealed to me that morning. I put the verse in my purse as I headed out the door to an appointment with my husband. As we were driving, I received a call from our daughter. She was a high school student at the time. One of her dear friends had been struggling with rebellion. Her parents were frustrated and had told her the night before that they were going to take her out of the local high school and send her to live with her grandparents. They had tried everything and were ready to take drastic action.

Our daughter asked if I would come to the school to talk to her friend. We turned around and headed for the high school. The office personnel allowed us to meet in one of the offices. As I listened to Hailey's (not her real name) struggle, the Lord brought Deuteronomy 13:4 to my mind. Suddenly, I knew that the verse was for her! I began to share it with her and encourage her to follow God's Word to avoid the traps of the evil one. God granted "a word of wisdom" (1 Cor. 12:8) as I shared and tears streamed down her face. I was able to pray with her and left knowing it had been a divine appointment.

That afternoon, I drove up to the high school to pick up our younger daughter from cheerleading practice. I saw Hailey's father waiting. I walked over to his car to let him know that I had talked with Hailey that morning. Tears came to his eyes as he said, "I was talking to her grandmother this morning and told her how much I wished Hailey could talk to you." God answered the desire of this father's heart and prepared me for the assignment during my morning time with the Lord.

A couple of weeks later, I sent a new Christian CD to school with my daughter to give to Hailey. She checked out of school to go home for something and put the CD in her car stereo. Before she could make it to her house, she pulled over on the side of the road and wept as she cried out to God for salvation!

Our God is intimately acquainted with our ways. He is involved in the details. As we submit to the promptings of His Spirit, He will accomplish the extraordinary through what may appear to be very ordinary actions on our behalf.

What if I had missed my time that morning? What if I had not valued that time and had allowed other pressing issues and the busyness of the day to steal that time from me? I know the Lord can use us even when we miss our prayer time. But I was especially prepared with a word from God that fit Hailey's situation because God had spoken to me during my time with Him.

Calvin Miller noted our busyness and fascination with the clock. He stated:

> This has led us to bizarre forms of relating to God through the Holy Spirit. We run into the prayer room, into the very throne of God—slam down our prayer demands and run out again so that we can be on time for our next appointment. But the Holy Spirit wants us to know that God is not some fast-food supplier

of our "McPrayerlife." He is the unhurried Jehovah who treasures those wonderful moments of leisure that we freely give Him.[4]

Just as I have a commitment to a systematic plan for reading through the Bible, I have found it helpful to have a plan for recording prayer requests and the verses God uses to speak to me. I use a simple three-ring binder as a prayer notebook. I have dividers for each section. My sections are:

1. Praise (scripture praises and thanksgiving)

2. Family (pictures and individual pages of requests and scripture prayers; clear page protectors work great for including pictures in your notebook)

3. Church (list of staff and scriptures prayed for my local body of Christ)

4. Friends (Christian friends and ministries)

5. Intercession (for the lost, sick, praying for a spouse, barren, etc.)

6. Government (local and national—leaders and spiritual needs)

7. World Atlas (missions and missionaries)

Obviously, you don't have to have a notebook like I do, but you do need to have a method to record requests and answers. My husband uses blank business cards to record requests. He has stacks of cards that he prays through. He also memorizes scripture on business cards and prays many of them back to the Lord. I have a friend who uses a prayer journal that she renews each year.

It really doesn't matter how you organize your prayer time. Find a method that works for you and stick with it. One of the greatest faith-building activities you can do is to look back in your prayer notebook and review the answers to prayer that God has granted.

When God speaks to you through a verse during your Bible reading, record it in your prayer notebook. Many times God will speak to you about a specific prayer request as you are reading. Write that verse down and begin to pray it back to the Lord with that request.

> Our faith is not in our ability to believe but in God's faithfulness to His Word.

As parents, Steve and I have interceded hours for our children. We didn't want to simply raise good children but wanted to raise godly children—passionate pursuers of Christ. Passion for God is caught more than it is taught. We both have many verses that we have prayed for our children through the years. Three of our four children are married and having children of their own. We have lived long enough to see many of these scripture promises fulfilled by our Lord. God's Word does not return void (Isa. 55:11 KJV). Stand on the scriptures through which He has spoken to you, and do not allow doubt or discouragement to defeat your faith. Our faith is not in our ability to believe but in God's faithfulness to His Word.

One of the most convincing proofs of the existence of God is the evidence of Him in your life. Your children may run from God, but they should never be able to truthfully deny His existence because they have seen the supernatural evidence of Him in your prayer life. Your personal prayer life should be anything but ordinary!

I have long loved John 15 and Christ's analogy of Himself as the vine and us as branches. Jesus made it very clear that we could do nothing apart from Him (v. 5). It is as we abide in Christ that we enter in and begin to pray according to His will. Only then will we "bear much fruit, and so prove to be [His] disciples" (v. 8 NASB). If you look at the context of this verse, you will find that the proof of our discipleship (belonging to Christ) is answered prayer!

QUESTIONS TO CONSIDER

1. Decide on a system for recording your prayer requests and God's answers.

2. Share a recent answer to prayer with one of your family members or friends.

★ ★ ★

Reflect on the following testimony and determine to begin praying with others from whom you can learn and grow.

PRAYER IS A LANGUAGE LEARNED
Joni's Story

In the beginning of our relationship with God, we come to prayer simply, with our wilderness words and a longing to be heard. We falter at first, often uttering only a word or two—*help*, *please*, *why*, or *thank you*. Like all new language learners, we grow in the language of prayer best by immersion, by listening to native speakers, by imitating what we hear, and by practicing independently so our thoughts take prayer shape more easily.

My daughter once asked me, "How did you learn to pray?" My answer was simple: I learned to pray by praying with others.

At first, much of my learning was passive. As a child, I listened to my parents and my grandma pray. As an adult, I went to Bible study and I listened intently to others praying. Like an infant, I took it all in, wide-eyed sometimes at the boldness and confidence of the words. After a few months, I took an active learning path, joining a group of women who met before Bible study to pray. Here I offered my first prayers aloud, feeling as much a babbler as my toddlers in the nursery down the hall. To my surprise, my babbling was celebrated, not corrected. With others, I learned to ask God to do what only He could do. And I watched as He did just that.

The next few years brought new lessons. I spent time with a friend and spiritual mentor, learning to pray on the way, in her black van as we drove to necessary places, in restaurants as she asked the servers if she could pray for their needs, at kitchen tables as we shared our own needs, and across the ocean as we followed God to the physical and spiritual needs of others. She was the first to model how to use God's own written words to help form my prayers, to shape my desires. I learned from special friends that prayer can bring healing to the past as well as the present. And I began to learn that prayer is as much about listening as speaking.

It has been almost two decades since those first Bible study days. I'm learning to pray still.

This book in your hands is evidence that you, too, desire to learn the language of prayer. Listen to others pray. Read the prayers of David in the Psalms, read the prayers of Jesus in the Gospels, and read the prayers of Paul in his New Testament letters. Continue to read the prayer stories in this book. Imitate what you hear. Babble. Practice. Pray with others. Listen. Learn to minister to God in prayer. Keep learning to pray.

I'm learning with you.

~ NOTES ~

CHAPTER TWENTY

THE ARK OF THE COVENANT

REVEALING AND TRANSFORMING

For Jesus is not some high priest who has no sympathy
for our weaknesses *and flaws*. He has already been
tested in every way that we are tested; but He
emerged victorious, without failing God. So let us
step boldly to the throne of grace, where we can
find mercy and grace to help when we need it most.

–Hebrews 4:15-16

May God open our eyes to see what
the holy ministry of intercession is,
to which, as His royal priesthood,
we have been set apart.

–Andrew Murray[1]

The veil of Christ's body has been torn (Heb. 10:20), and we
have been invited in. We may now enter confidently (with freedom
of speech) before the very throne of God. The throne of judgment

has now become a throne of mercy and grace (2 Kings 19:15; Ps. 99:1; Isa. 6: Heb. 4:16; Rev. 4)!

God paid the price and made the way that we might know Him and enjoy Him forever. In her book *Power in the Name of Jesus,* Jennifer Kennedy Dean states, "So the conclusion is this: God has provided the way into holiness. He has provided the way into His Presence, where there is fullness of joy. He has accomplished everything for us so that we can live in an eternal Sabbath. We have partaken of the cup of sanctification that He poured out and offered to us."[2]

> God has provided the way into holiness. He has provided the way into His Presence, where there is fullness of joy.
>
> –Jennifer Kennedy Dean

This reality drives me to my knees. As I kneel, I like to envision the scene so beautifully described in Revelation 4–5. The throne depicted there is the very mercy seat before which I kneel. Obviously, it isn't a requirement to kneel, but I can hardly imagine this scene without bowing before the One who sits enthroned upon that seat. Oh, the majesty and glory and holiness of my God. How rich are His grace and mercy toward those who believe.

The good news of the gospel is that I will not be consumed or knocked off my feet when I stand before Him one day. Because I am "in Christ" I will be able to stand. "Standing in His presence, by faith, we are unafraid; our souls shall never die; for the broken law is covered by His precious blood. And one day we shall see Him 'face to face'—to worship Him forever for His unspeakable love!"[3]

Hallelujah! The law is covered with the blood of His grace and mercy! "Mercy and truth are met together; righteousness and peace have kissed each other" (Ps. 85:10 KJV).

When I was teaching through the Bible at the women's conference in New Delhi, India, and God revealed His truth about the Tree of Life, I had another significant revelation. As I read Revelation 22:4, "They will be able to look upon His face," I was struck by my desire to reach out and cup His face with my hands—the face that I have loved since I was a nine-year-old girl. Now, I am aware that when I see His face, I will fall on *my* face. But for that moment, my first response was to reach out and touch the One who has loved me so perfectly. I was astounded by His mercy and the intimacy of that moment. I am His and He is mine! The blood of His mercy has covered the law, and I am accepted, beloved, and one with my Savior!

When we believe and are seeking God through His Word and prayer, He reveals kingdom truths to us. We begin to view the world and our cities as places for which we are responsible. As we intercede for our cities (Jer. 29:7), God will begin to bless those cities and use us to take the love and light of Christ into the darkness.

We now live and minister in my hometown, Memphis, Tennessee. Memphis is known for many things: Elvis Presley, barbecue, the blues, the Mississippi River, dogwoods and azaleas, and for being the home of FedEx. Unfortunately, we are also known as the city with the fifth highest violent crime rate,[4] high teen pregnancy rates, high unemployment, inner-city poverty, and a struggling school system currently consolidating city and county schools.

Our church began quarterly "mission trips" into the city in 2007. We call these service days "Bellevue Loves Memphis," based on Jeremiah 29:7—"Seek the welfare of the city where I have sent you into exile, and pray to the LORD on its behalf; for in its welfare you will have welfare" (NASB).

These service days have provided opportunities for our church to "be Jesus" as we have repaired inner-city school football fields and teacher lounges, and done landscaping and general cleanup around the schools. We have picked up trash, painted and repaired inner-city churches, installed ramps for the disabled, and repaired widows' homes. We have a ministry in north Memphis, where I grew up, that serves some of the most economically challenged people in our city. Our food bank and the local church minister to the community on a daily basis.

Our church purchased a mobile dental clinic that provides free dental care to the needy in our city. Dentists and dental hygienists from across the city volunteer their time to provide these services.

Through these projects, Sunday school classes and individuals have taken on their own projects that they do on a more frequent basis. One young adult class asked for a plot of ground on the back-side of our church property. They planted a garden and harvested four thousand pounds of vegetables that were given away to the Memphis Food Bank and our ministry in Frayser. It has been a wonderful way for these families with children to serve together and make a difference in our city.

After serving in our city for a couple of years, I became burdened for the children. I started going to the inner city to tutor with my niece and a few of her friends one afternoon a week. As a former educator, I know the importance of children having early success in elementary school. In her book *Educating All God's Children*, Nicole Baker Fulgham said, "On average, students in low-income communities are three grade levels behind their peers in affluent communities by the time they are in fourth grade." She goes on to say, "The educational achievement gap arguably represents the United States' most blatant and chilling example of neglect."[5]

As I was praying about how to better reach the large numbers of our children in the city, the Lord seemed to shake me with these words: *"This is your city. These are your children. What are you doing about it?"*

I called one of our staff members who serves as our liaison between our church and the schools that we have been serving. I asked her how we needed to proceed to help assist our school district and possibly encourage the churches in our city to adopt these schools.

She called the volunteer coordinator, who was thrilled about our interest! She said the school board had told her they wanted her to increase the number of faith-based organizations that adopted schools. We asked her to send us a list of the schools and their needs.

She forwarded us a list of Priority Schools in the state of Tennessee. These are the schools that are functioning below the state's minimum standards. There were eighty-three schools on the list, and sixty-nine of them were in our city. Thirty-two of them were elementary schools. Ten of these elementary schools had already been taken over by the state and were going to be run by a charter school company. So we decided to focus on the other twenty-two.

God has done "exceeding abundantly above" (KJV) anything we could have ever imagined (Eph. 3:20)! The Lord has opened doors and ignited a passion for our schools in the hearts of many of our churches and organizations. We are coming together to adopt

> "This is your city. These are your children. What are you doing about it?"
>
> —God

schools, provide tutors focusing on K–3, and partner with churches in the communities to minister to the entire family.

We are partnering with other ministries to reach children from the womb to adulthood. We began praying and working in August 2012. By November we had a meeting with four national ministries that had selected Memphis to pilot their programs and wanted to partner with us. A friend and women's ministry director from another church and I looked at each other with jaws dropped and marveled that God had put together such a great team in such a short amount of time.

> It is time for the body of Christ to join hands across denominational and racial lines and be the Body!

Since that meeting we have had days of training for volunteers. Churches are coming on board. God supernaturally put me in meetings to talk to our governor's wife, Crissy Haslam, who has a desire to reach the children of our state, and Nicole Baker Fulgham, author of *Educating All God's Children*, who desires to do on a national scale what we are seeking to do in Memphis.

God has given us a focal scripture—Psalm 78:6–7, "That the generation to come might know, even the children yet to be born, that they may **arise** and tell them to their children, that they should put their confidence in God, and not forget the works of God, but keep His commandments" (NASB; emphasis added). Thus, ARISE Memphis was born. (ARISE stands for **A R**enewal **I**n **S**tudent **E**ducation and Evangelism. See www.arisememphis.org.)

Our goal is to have all of the twenty-two elementary school (K–3) classes adopted by a church or Sunday school class. We want tutors spending at least one hour each week with these students and focusing on helping them be on grade level in reading and math by third grade.

The adopter schools will be partnering with a local church (community church) and assisting them to meet the needs of their neighborhood families. We are partnering with pro-life ministries, One by One (mentoring for expectant moms for the first year to two years of the child's life), the Fatherhood Initiative, and Evan-Tell. We serve to meet needs and share the gospel. It will be of no benefit if we create a successful school district and cleaner neighborhoods from which these families die apart from Christ and enter a Christless eternity. Our mandate from Christ is to "make disciples" (Matt. 28:19–20).

It is time for the body of Christ to join hands across denominational and racial lines and be the Body! Evangelical churches need to partner with one another and take the light of the gospel to a world that is perishing. Jesus said, "Your love for one another will prove to the world that you are my disciples" (John 13:35 NLT).

Once we began following the lead of the Holy Spirit with ARISE Memphis, God brought people alongside us to help us get organized, create a website, visit potential adopter churches, and recruit volunteers to tutor.

The previous five years of concentrated prayer and service for our city is reaping a great harvest. There is still much to do, but God is moving so quickly that we are just trying to keep up! As we walk with Him, He is showing us the way, providing our needs, and granting us rest as we depend upon Him.

It seems that everywhere I turn, God is confirming His call. As believers we are called to care for the "least of these" (Matt. 25:40 KJV). I can tell you, I would not be able to sleep at night if I thought my children or grandchildren were hungry or didn't have the things they needed for school. Should I care any less for the children of my city who go to bed hungry at night?

As we were preparing for one of our first luncheons to introduce ARISE to some of the churches in our city, our women's ministry director received a poem by e-mail. It spoke directly to the heart of the issue and is something I would ask that you read prayerfully.

A PRAYER FOR CHILDREN

We pray for children
> who give us sticky kisses,
> who hop rocks and chase butterflies,
> who stomp in puddles and ruin their new
>> pants,
> who sneak Popsicles before supper,
> who erase holes in math workbooks,
> who can never find their shoes.

And we pray for those
> who stare at photographers from behind
>> barbed wire,
> who've never squeaked across the floor in new
>> sneakers,
> who've never "counted potatoes,"
> who are born in places we wouldn't be caught
>> dead,
> who never go to the circus,
> who live in an X-rated world.

We pray for children
> who bring us fistfuls of dandelions and sing
>> off-key,

who have goldfish funerals, build card-table
    forts,
who slurp their cereal on purpose,
who get gum in their hair, put sugar in their
    milk,
who spit toothpaste all over the sink,
who hug us for no reason, who bless us each
    night.
And we pray for those
    who never get dessert,
    who watch their parents watch them die,
    who have no safe blanket to drag behind,
    who can't find any bread to steal,
    who don't have any rooms to clean up,
    whose pictures aren't on anybody's dresser,
    whose monsters are real.
We pray for children
    who spend all their allowance before Tuesday,
    who throw tantrums in the grocery store
    and pick at their food,
    who like ghost stories,
    who shove dirty clothes under the bed
    and never rinse out the tub,
    who get quarters from the tooth fairy,
    who don't like to be kissed in front of the car
        pool,
    who squirm in church and scream in the
        phone,
    whose tears we sometimes laugh at
    and whose smiles can make us cry.

And we pray for those

    whose nightmares come in the daytime,

    who will eat anything,

    who have never seen a dentist,

    who aren't spoiled by anybody,

    who go to bed hungry and cry themselves to

        sleep,

    who live and move, but have no being.

We pray for children

    who want to be carried,

    and for those who must.

    For those we never give up on,

    and for those who don't have a chance.

    For those we smother,

    and for those who will grab the hand of

        anybody

    kind enough to offer.

        —Ina J. Hughs[6]

Are you willing to offer a hand? What is God doing through you as a direct result of your prayers? Are your prayers impacting your city, country, and the world? Remember, dear friend, prayer is not preparation for the battle; prayer *is* the battle!

It is only as we are filled with His Spirit, and allow Him to strengthen us and lead us, that we will be able to advance the kingdom of God. We cannot do this in the flesh! The enemy is much too strong and our abilities too feeble to accomplish God's plan. He must be living in and through us.

When God moves in answer to prayer, and it is obvious that His hand has accomplished it, He receives all the glory! He will share His glory with no one (Isa. 42:8). We are to follow the example of Christ, who "did not come to be served, but to serve, and to give His life a ransom for many" (Matt. 20:28 NKJV). Are you giving your life away for the gospel?

May His glory be manifest in our lives just as it was in the tabernacle built by the Israelites. Join me in praying along with Andrew Murray:

> Ever-blessed Father, be pleased, I beseech Thee, to open the eyes of Thy children to the vision that even as Thy Son was perfected for evermore, so Thou art waiting to work in each of us that work of perfecting Thy saints in which Thy glory will be seen.[7]

QUESTIONS TO CONSIDER

1. How has the knowledge that you stand before the throne of grace affected your life?

2. What are you doing to live out your new life in Christ?

3. Consider ways in which you might minister to those in need. What are you doing now? What could you do?

NOTES

APPENDIX

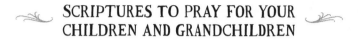

SCRIPTURES TO PRAY FOR YOUR CHILDREN AND GRANDCHILDREN

I pray that my children will love the Lord with all their hearts, souls, minds, and strength. **(based on Mark 12:30)**

I pray that my children will grow as Jesus did—"Jesus kept increasing in wisdom and stature, and in favor with God and men." **(Luke 2:52 NASB)**

I pray that my children will "grow in grace, and in the knowledge of our Lord and Saviour Jesus Christ." **(2 Peter 3:18 KJV)**

I pray that my children will lean not on their own understanding, but in all their ways they will acknowledge You, and You will direct their paths. **(based on Proverbs 3:5–6)**

I pray that my children will "honor all people, love the brotherhood, fear God, honor the king." **(1 Peter 2:17 NASB)**

I pray that my children will seek first Your kingdom and Your righteousness, and the other things they need will be added to them. **(based on Matthew 6:33)**

May my children know that You have not given them a spirit of fear but of power and love and a sound mind, or discipline. **(based on 2 Timothy 1:7)**

Lord, clothe my children with the virtue of compassion. **(based on Colossians 3:12)**

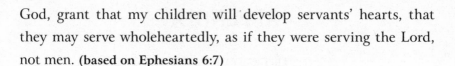

God, grant that my children will develop servants' hearts, that they may serve wholeheartedly, as if they were serving the Lord, not men. **(based on Ephesians 6:7)**

Lord, teach my children to pray. **(based on Luke 11:1)**

May their souls long for You as the deer pants for the water brooks. **(based on Psalm 42:1 NASB)**

I pray that my children will be filled with joy because of You and will sing praises to Your name, O Most High. **(based on Psalm 9:2 NLT)**

I pray You will show my children the way of life, granting them the joy of Your presence and the pleasures of living with You forever. **(based on Psalm 16:11)**

I pray that all of my children will be taught of the Lord and that their well-being will be great. **(based on Isaiah 54:13)**

I pray my children will prosper and be in good health even as their souls prosper. **(based on 3 John 2)**

I pray my children will be "filled with the Spirit." **(Ephesians 5:18 NASB)**

Lord, I pray my children will present their bodies to you as living sacrifices, holy and acceptable, which is their spiritual service of worship. I pray that they will not be conformed to this world, but be transformed by the renewing of their minds, that they may prove what the will of God is, that which is good, acceptable, and perfect. **(based on Romans 12:1–2)**

I pray You will manifest the fruit of Your Spirit in _____'s life—"love, joy, peace, patience, kindness, goodness, faithfulness, gentleness, self-control; against such things there is no law." **(Galatians 5:22–23** NASB**)**

I pray that this book of the law shall not depart from _____'s mouth, but that he/she shall meditate on it day and night, so that _____ may be careful to do according to all that is written in it; for then You will make _____'s way prosperous, and then _____ will have success." **(based on Joshua 1:8** NASB**)**

Father, I thank you for your covenant: "'As for Me, this is My covenant with them,' says the LORD: 'My Spirit which is upon you, and My words which I have put in your mouth shall not depart from your mouth, nor from the mouth of your offspring, nor from the mouth of your offspring's offspring,' says the LORD, 'from now and forever.'" **(Isaiah 59:21** NASB**)**

Oh that You would bless [child's name] indeed and enlarge his/her border, and that Your hand might be with _____, and that You would keep _____ from harm that it may not pain him/her! **(based on 1 Chronicles 4:10** NASB**)**

> How blessed is the man who does not walk in the
>   counsel of the wicked,
> Nor stand in the path of sinners,
> Nor sit in the seat of scoffers!
> But his delight is in the law of the LORD,
>   And in His law he meditates day and night.
> He will be like a tree firmly planted by streams of
>   water,
> Which yields its fruit in its season
> And its leaf does not wither;

And in whatever he does, he prospers. (Psalm 1:1–3 NASB)

FOR DAUGHTERS AND GRANDDAUGHTERS

"Charm is deceitful and beauty is vain, but a woman who fears the LORD, she shall be praised." **(Proverbs 31:30 NASB)**

SCRIPTURES TO PRAY FOR YOUR HUSBAND

"For it is You who blesses the righteous man, O LORD, You surround him with favor as with a shield." **(Psalm 5:12 NASB)**

In the morning O Lord, you will hear _____'s voice; in the morning he will order his prayer to Thee and eagerly watch. **(based on Psalm 5:3)**

I pray that _____ will be as shrewd as a serpent and as innocent as a dove. **(based on Matthew 10:16)**

I pray that _____ will care for his family as David cared for Israel: "He cared for them with a true heart and led them with skillful hands." **(Psalm 78:72 NLT)**

I pray, Lord, that you will hear _____'s voice in accordance with Your love. **(based on Psalm 119:149 NIV)**

Surely goodness and mercy shall follow _____ all the days of his life; and he will dwell in the house of the Lord forever. **(based on Psalm 23:6 NKJV)**

May _____ prosper and be in good health even as his soul prospers. **(based on 3 John 2)**

The following scripture prayers were taken from a prayer card by FamilyLife Publishing, titled "Lifting My Husband Through Prayer." The verses quoted are from the English Standard Version (ESV).

Fill my husband with love for you, that he would love you "with all [his] heart and with all [his] soul and with all [his] mind (Matthew 22:37–40).

Place his "delight . . . in the law of the LORD" (Psalm 1:2), and "open [his] eyes that [he] may behold wondrous things out of your law" (Psalm 119:18). Give him understanding (Psalm 119:73).

Compel him to pray continually (1 Thessalonians 5:17) so that he'll live and walk by your Spirit (Galatians 5:25).

Empower him to "run with endurance the race that is set before [him]" and to focus on pleasing you (Hebrews 12:1–2).

Equip my husband with strength and wisdom to lead, that he would be "strong and very courageous," and that he may be successful wherever he goes (Joshua 1:7).

Supply him the time and ability to "manage his own household well" (1 Timothy 3:4).

Guide him in using wisely all the resources you've given us, keeping an eternal perspective about possessions (Matthew 6:19–21; Luke 16:10–13).

May he share your hatred of evil and experience your protection (**Psalm 97:10**).

Enable him to be "quick to hear, slow to speak, slow to anger" (**James 1:19**).

Help him to trust you "with all [his] heart, and [not to] lean on [his] own understanding." Make his paths straight (**Proverbs 3:5**).

Flood him with peace and faith (**Isaiah 26:3; John 14:1**).

Increase his desire to teach and model godliness as a father, "that the next generation might know . . . and not forget the works of God" (**Psalm 78:5–7**).

Because you oppose the proud and give grace to the humble (**James 4:6**), instill a genuine sense of humility in my husband's heart (**see also Isaiah 66:2**).

Keep him sexually pure and honorable. "Blessed are the pure in heart, for they shall see God" (**Matthew 5:8; see also 1 Corinthians 6:18–20**).

Give him friendships with godly men (**Proverbs 27:17**), that they would "stir up one another to love and good works" (**Hebrews 10:24**).

Let your favor rest upon him, and "establish the work of [his] hands" (**Psalm 90:17**).[1]

SUGGESTED VERSES FOR
MEMORIZATION

Psalm 1:1–3

Proverbs 3:5–6

Proverbs 18:10

Proverbs 28:13

Proverbs 31:30–31

Isaiah 26:3

Isaiah 41:10

Isaiah 53:4–6

Isaiah 55:8–11

Isaiah 64:4

Jeremiah 7:23–24

Luke 9:23

John 2:1–2

Romans 3:23

Romans 8:28

Romans 15:4–5

1 Corinthians 6:9–11

1 Corinthians 10:13

Galatians 5:22–23

Ephesians 3:20–21

Ephesians 6:10–18

Philippians 4:6–7

Colossians 3:1–4

Colossians 3:16–17

2 Timothy 3:16

Titus 3:5–6

Hebrews 11:1, 6

2 Peter 3:9

1 John 2:1–2

NOTES

PART ONE INTRODUCTION

1. Henry Nouwen, *The Selfless Way of Christ: Downward Mobility and the Spiritual Life* (Maryknoll, NY: Orbis, 2007), 75.

CHAPTER 1

1. Denise George, *A Longing Heart Hears God's Gentle Whisper* (Lynnwood, WA: Aglow, 1993), 93.
2. Edward Welch, *Shame Interrupted: How God Lifts the Pain and Worthlessness of Rejection* (Greensboro, NC: New Growth Press, 2012), 46.

CHAPTER 2

1. Oswald Chambers, *The Best from All His Books*, vol. 2, ed. Harry Verploegh (Nashville: Thomas Nelson, 1989), 232.
2. Charles Caldwell Ryrie, *Ryrie Study Bible* (Chicago: Moody Press, 1978), 29.
3. Chambers, *The Best from All His Books*, 86.

CHAPTER 4

1. Stephen F. Olford, *The Tabernacle: Camping with God* (Grand Rapids: Kregel, 2004), 17.
2. F. B. Meyer, *The Way into the Holiest: Expositions of the Epistle to the Hebrews* (New York: Fleming H. Revell, 1893), 140.
3. Olford, *The Tabernacle*, 27.
4. E. M. Bounds, *The Classic Collection on Prayer*, ed. Harold Chadwick (Alachua, FL: Bridge-Logos, 2001), 221.

CHAPTER 5

1. Mark D. Thompson, *A Clear and Present Word: The Clarity of Scripture* (Downers Grove, IL: InterVarsity Press, 2006), 162–63.
2. Betty Vick, notes from lecture, Memphis, TN.
3. Brennan Manning, *The Relentless Tenderness of Jesus* (Grand Rapids: Revell, 2004), 67–68.

CHAPTER 6

1. Stephen F. Olford, *The Tabernacle: Camping with God* (Grand Rapids: Kregel, 2004), 78.
2. Martin Luther, in *The Westminster Collection of Christian Quotations*, comp. Martin H. Manser (Louisville: WJK Books, 2001), 37.

3. Nancy Leigh DeMoss, *Surrender: The Heart God Controls* (Chicago: Moody, 2003), 54.
4. Manley Beasley Sr., *Faith Workbook*, vol. 1, for Beasley, *Faith Is Now*, created and donated by John R. Wills, http://www.manleybeasley.com/Faith%20WorkBook%20Volume%201.pdf, 4.

CHAPTER 7

1. Louis Talbot, *Christ in the Tabernacle* (Los Angeles: The Bible Institute, 1942), Kindle edition, chap. 7.
2. Gary Smalley, *Making Love Last Forever* (Nashville: W Publishing Group, 1996), 162, 173.
3. Ibid., 162, 174.
4. Ibid., 162, 173–74.
5. Bob Sorge, *Secrets of the Secret Place: Keys to Igniting Your Personal Time with God* (Greenwood, MO: Oasis House, 2001), 62.

CHAPTER 8

1. Watchman Nee, *The Release of the Spirit* (Indianapolis: Sure Foundation, 1965), 72.
2. M. R. DeHaan, *The Tabernacle* (Grand Rapids: Zondervan, 1983), 97–98.
3. Ibid., 100.

CHAPTER 9

1. Spiros Zodhiates, ed., *Hebrew-Greek Key Study Bible* (Chattanooga: AMG, 1990), 113.
2. David M. Levy, *The Tabernacle: Shadows of the Messiah* (Bellmawr, NJ: Friends of Israel Gospel Ministry, Inc., 1993), 26.
3. Devi Titus, *The Table Experience: Discover What Creates Deeper, More Meaningful Relationships* (Oviedo, FL: HigherLife Development Services, Inc., 2009), 26.
4. Ibid., 27.
5. Ibid., 10.
6. Ibid., 11.
7. Henri Nouwen, *The Selfless Way of Christ: Downward Mobility and the Spiritual Life* (Maryknoll, NY: Orbis, 2007), 78.

CHAPTER 10

1. Steve Gaines, *Pray Like It Matters* (Tigerville, SC: Auxano Press, 2013), 23.
2. Bob Sorge, *Secrets of the Secret Place: Keys to Igniting Your Personal Time with God* (Greenwood, MO: Oasis House, 2001), 4.
3. Oswald Chambers, *The Best from All His Books*, vol. 2, ed. Harry Verploegh (Nashville: Thomas Nelson, 1989), 243.

CHAPTER 11

1. John S. Barnett, *Pathway to the Most High: The Tabernacle Mysteries for Today* (n.p.: BFM Books, 2009), Kindle edition, loc. 392.
2. David M. Levy, *The Tabernacle: Shadows of the Messiah* (Bellmawr, NJ: Friends of Israel Gospel Ministry, Inc., 1993), 72.
3. Jennifer Kennedy Dean, *Power in the Name of Jesus* (Birmingham: New Hope, 2012), 153.

CHAPTER 14

1. N. T. Wright, *Acts* (Downers Grove, IL: InterVarsity Press, 2010),13.
2. Tim Keller, *The Prodigal God* (New York: Dutton, 2008), 105.
3. G. K. Beale, *The Temple and the Church's Mission: A Biblical Theology of the Dwelling Place of God* (Downers Grove, IL: InterVarsity Press, 2004), 369.

CHAPTER 15

1. Dietrich Bonhoeffer, *The Cost of Discipleship* (New York: Touchstone, 1959), 11.
2. Brother Lawrence, *The Practice of the Presence of God* (New Kensington, PA: Whitaker House, 1982), 46.
3. George Barna, *Growing True Disciples: New Strategies for Producing Genuine Followers of Christ* (Colorado Springs: WaterBrook Press, 2001), 98–99.
4. Spiros Zodhiates, ed., *Hebrew-Greek Key Study Bible* (Chattanooga: AMG, 1990), 1716.
5. Howard G. Hendricks, *The Battle of the Gods* (Chicago: Moody Press, 1972), 41.

CHAPTER 16

1. Betty Vick, notes from lecture, Memphis, TN.
2. Reuben A. Olson, Robert L. Thomas, Peter P. Ahn, and W. Don Wilkins, eds./ *Zondervan NASB Exhaustive Concordance* (Grand Rapids: Zondervan, 2000), 1449.
3. Matthew Henry, *Matthew Henry Commentary* (2013), retrieved from BibleStudyTools.com, Psalm 37:4, http://www.biblestudytools.com/commentaries/matthew-henry-complete/psalms/37.html.
4. Dietrich Bonhoeffer, *The Cost of Discipleship* (New York: Touchstone, 1959), 215.
5. See "How to Memorize Scripture," The Navigators website, http://www.navigators.org/Tools/Discipleship%20Resources/Tools/Topical%20Memory%20System

CHAPTER 17

1. Spiros Zodhiates, ed., *Hebrew-Greek Key Study Bible*, "Greek Dictionary of the New Testament" (Chattanooga: AMG, 1990), 54.

2. See Chronological Bible Teaching website. http://www. chronologicalbibleteaching.com/training/.
3. Andrew Murray, *Prayer Power* (New Kensington, PA: Whitaker House, 1998), 57.
4. Calvin Miller, *Loving God Up Close: Rekindling Your Relationship with the Holy Spirit* (n.p.: Warner Faith, 2004), 45.

CHAPTER 18

1. Ann Voskamp, "The Best Way to Handle Hunger Cravings {The Pumpkin Cannon Edition: Fridays on the Farm}," *A Holy Experience* (blog), September 28, 2012, http://www.aholyexperience.com/2012/09/ the-best-way-to-handle-hunger-cravings-the-pumpkin-cannon-edition- fridays-on-the-farm/.
2. See (in order of the names of Christ) John 10:7; Revelation 5:12; John 15:3; Hebrews 4:12–13; John 8:12; Ephesians 5:18; John 6:35; Hebrews 7:25; 1 John 2:1; Hebrews 10:20; Hebrews 9:24–25; Luke 2:11; Philippians 3:8; Luke 17:13; Matthew 16:16; Mark 9:31.
3. Sylvia Gunter, *Prayers for the Family* (Hoover, AL: Alpha Graphics, 1994), 14.
4. David Lee Martin, *Tabernacle Prayer: An Interactive Guide to Tabernacle and Temple Prayer* (JesusChrist.co.uk, 2013), Kindle edition, loc. 477.
5. A.W. Tozer, *The Pursuit of God* (Camp Hill, PA: Christian Publications, 1993), 77.

CHAPTER 19

1. Samuel Chadwick, *The Path of Prayer* (Jawbone Digital, 2012) loc. 738–39.
2. Helen Lemmel, "Turn Your Eyes upon Jesus," 1922, *The Cyber Hymnal*, http://cyberhymnal.org/htm/t/u/turnyour.htm.
3. Jeanne Guyon, *Experiencing Union with God Through Prayer* (Gainesville, FL: Bridge-Logos, 2001), 144.
4. Calvin Miller, *Loving God Up Close: Rekindling Your Relationship with the Holy Spirit* (n.p.: Warner Faith, 2004), 121.

CHAPTER 20

1. Andrew Murray, *The Wisdom of Andrew Murray,* vol. 1 (Radford, VA: Wilder, 2008), 63.
2. Jennifer Kennedy Dean, *Power in the Name of Jesus* (Birmingham: New Hope, 2012), 151.
3. Louis Talbot, *Christ in the Tabernacle* (Los Angeles: The Bible Institute, 1942), Kindle edition, loc. 2153.
4. Jane Donahoe, "Violent crime database: Where does Memphis stand?," *Memphis Business Journal*, February 7, 2013. http://www.bizjournals.com/ memphis/news/2013/02/07/violent-crime-database-where-does.html.

5. Nicole Baker Fulgham, *Educating All God's Children* (Grand Rapids: Brazos Press, 2013), 24, 16.
6. Ina J. Hughs, "A Prayer for Children" from *A Prayer for Children* copyright © 1995 by Ina Hughs. Used by permission of HarperCollins Publishers, XIV–XV.
7. Andrew Murray, *The Secret of the Faith Life* (Fort Washington, PA: CLC, 1998), Twenty-Eighth Day.

APPENDIX

1. "Lifting My Husband Through Prayer" prayer card (Little Rock: FamilyLife Publishing, 2010), www.FamilyLife.com.

ABOUT THE AUTHOR

Donna Gaines has discovered the transforming power a surrendered life and a hungry heart bring to her own life. As a pastor's wife, Bible teacher, and disciple maker, she passionately communicates the truth of God's Word to women and challenges them to live out their high call in Christ Jesus. Embracing God's missional calling on her life, Donna mobilizes women to practically live out the global implications of their faith through both inner city and international efforts. The author of two books, *There's Gotta Be More* and *Seated: Living from Our Position in Christ,* Donna is also the editor of *A Daily Women's Devotional.* She is married to Dr. Steve Gaines, pastor of Bellevue Baptist Church. Known as "Mom" to her son and three daughters and "Nonna" to her six grandchildren, Donna enjoys Memphis bar-b-que, Alabama football, and anything that you can douse with salsa.

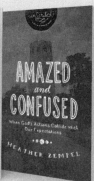

SHARE THE INSCRIBED COLLECTION

EXPERIENCE THE BOOKS

Your friends can sample this book or any of our InScribed titles for FREE. Visit InScribedStudies.com and select any of our titles to learn how.

Know a church, ministry, or small group that would benefit from these readings? Contact your favorite bookseller or visit InScribedStudies.com/buy-in-bulk for bulk purchasing information.

CONNECT WITH THE AUTHORS

Do you want to get to know more about the author of this book or any of the authors in the InScribed Collection? Go online to InScribedStudies.com to see how you could meet them through a Google Hangout or connect with them through our InScribed Facebook.

JOIN IN THE CONVERSATION

 Like facebook.com/InScribedStudies and be the first to see new videos, discounts, and updates from the InScribed Studies team.

 Start following @InScribedStudy.

 Follow our author's boards @InScribedStudies.

WWW.INSCRIBEDSTUDIES.COM

THOMAS NELSON
Since 1798